Fr

Norm y

with Picardy, Nord and Pas-de-Calais

Jarrold Publishing

CONTENTS

Title page: Honfleur

Introducing Normandy

Go south-west of Paris and you'll find Normandy! Only its southernmost fringes, of course – the area around Alençon. But this rather surprising fact is only one of many that Normandy, one of the great landscapes of France, has in store for you, even though few can be uncovered as easily, from just a glance at the map. Perhaps more than any other region of this vast country, Normandy needs to be experienced at first hand. Still relatively unknown, it is often lumped together with Brittany, if not actually confused with it. In the minds of many it is associated simply with the Second World War and the Allied landings on the Normandy coast – though even then people may not be too clear about where this coast begins and ends.

If you choose to take the coast road from the Belgian or northern French Channel ports you will find yourself being gradually prepared for Normandy by the scenery of Nord, the most northerly *département* in France. The succession of modest seaside resorts increases in elegance as you travel west, and the coastline begins to reveal more of its beauty, around Cap Gris-Nez for example (literally, Grey-Nose Point). Normandy itself, land of the Normans, begins near Le Tréport. Here, time and again, you will find the inhabitants insisting that they are Normans first and Frenchmen second – it's an idea they clearly like to flirt with even if they're not entirely serious about it. Indeed the three million Normans, most of whom live closer to England than to Paris, are wont to lay claim to their independence every bit as emphatically as any Breton or Provençal. Normandy is both the gateway to the Continent and its bulwark. Nowhere is history written more clearly than in the fortifications (some

Bayeux Cathedral

dating back almost 1,000 years) and in the great stone monuments to the region's piety – though where in the past they came in droves, today few pilgrims make the journey to Mont-St-Michel, the famous landmark on the border between Normandy and Brittany. At high tide an island soaring from the sea, at low water rising from the endless expanse of mud-flats, the Mount, with its transforming crown of abbey buildings, has become a symbol of France, even of the West.

North from Mont-St-Michel, the Cotentin peninsula has a rare tranquillity. You could almost be in Ireland – yellowy-grey walls, trees bowed by winds from the sea, and ruined churches from the early days of Christianity. So peaceful is it that you feel you can almost hear the clouds sailing across the dove-grey sky, the tides as they recede, and the soothing rain which seems to daub colour on the very grass and breathe slate-blue life into the low walls of rough quarry-stone. Here you can find a hotel room even in the high season, here the oysters taste their delicious best, and here the British Isles – in miniature in the shape of the Channel Islands – are closer to the French coast than at any other point.

Normandy's is a landscape of river and sea, of green expanses and gentle hills – hills often made higher by towering castles. The most famous of the castles, at Les Andelys and Gisors, had their roles to play in the story of Richard the Lionheart. But to reduce its attractions to just a few particular highlights does Normandy less than justice. Many parts of the sometimes precipitous, sometimes low-lying coast have special appeal, and a host of cathedrals and churches – all fine, and some among the very finest – hold court over the countryside. They also add character to some of the towns in the regions bordering Normandy to the east (included here as well), where cathedrals are the glory of cities such as Amiens, provincial capital of Picardy, and Laon – just 50 km from Reims.

One way to get to western Normandy from the northern Channel ports (if you are not intending to explore Nord) is to go to Rouen and take the motorway to Caen. (This could also be an appropriate route when the Channel Tunnel is open in a few years' time.) Traffic is generally not too heavy on the motorways; though not in fact as expensive as was originally feared, the motorway tolls *(péage)* are still enough to preserve a degree of exclusivity on France's uncomplicated network. This journey westwards brings you into contact with two major episodes in Normandy's history. Although the devastation of the Second World War is no longer visible in Caen itself, a recently opened museum on the city's outskirts – stage set, costume store and huge cinema rolled into one – graphically recalls the horrors of those days. And continuing west from Caen, you come to Bayeux, whose name inevitably brings to mind one of Normandy's most famous sons. The momentous voyage to England of

Memorial museum, Caen

William the Bastard in 1066 brought him the altogether more awe-inspiring title of 'the Conqueror' – as well as giving rise to the best-known work of Norman art, the embroidery we call the Bayeux Tapestry.

Anyone intent on getting the most out of a visit to Normandy will choose to avoid the high summer, preferring the months before or after, seasons of more subtle colouring and of empty hotels. It is usual to stay near the coast where the most interesting towns, the most enthralling scenery and the most glorious architecture are generally to be found, though as always there are some notable exceptions. Inevitably, however, the main focus of interest for most visitors will be northern Normandy, where the Seine follows its valley to the sea accompanied by a train of attendant abbeys and traversed by two bridges – the Pont de Tancarville and the Pont de Brotonne (1,400 m and 1,280 m long respectively) – suspension bridges which, with their twin 125-m-high pylons, set new engineering standards, both technical and aesthetic.

Holidays for everyone

Normandy incorporates a number of smaller, more manageable but naturally more limited sub-regions such as the Pays de Caux, the Pays d'Auge and the Suisse Normande – areas you can get to know, explore and 'conquer' with ease. Walking and cycling are not uncommon ways of going about it. Alternatively you can choose one of the towns or cities as your base – Rouen first and foremost, or Caen, or even Coutances at the neck of the Cotentin peninsula. However large or small the circle you then draw round it, you can be sure your chosen starting point will open the door to any number of colourful and varied holidays.

There is an abundance of sporting facilities almost everywhere. The horse became established in Normandy in Viking times, and there are horses all over the place today (perhaps the butchers dealing in horse meat, conspicuous by their numbers, also have something to do with it!). There are, therefore, many opportunities for riding. And in recent years several superb golf courses have been created, where large numbers of Parisians are to be found driving, pitching and putting in friendly rivalry with numerous English holidaymakers.

A holiday in northern climes can, of course, be quite different from a holiday in the sun: cooler weather, more wind, and the unpredictable dictates of sun and tide give – in comparison with the languor of continuous southern heat – a vastly different perspective to life on the beach. Favourable weather, though, isn't everything. You may need more in the way of planning and a lively curiosity but, after all, the great cathedrals were built here, not in the south. A holiday in northern France takes you among some of the most ancient as well as some of the most modern monuments to European history, into a countryside where you can learn to breathe properly once again, and along coasts where the power of untamed nature still makes its presence felt.

Crystalline rock and chalk cliffs

Uplands of modest height (and 600 million years old) are all the hill country Normandy has to offer, mainly in the south. West of Alençon, Mont des Avaloirs and Signal d'Ecouves (both 417 m) dispute the right to be called the highest. The

Right: St-Pierre and castle ramparts, Caen

crystalline rocks of the ancient Armorican Massif — slates alternating with granite and gneiss — stretch all the way from Brittany in the west to the Cotentin peninsula, before giving way to Jurassic limestone in the lower-lying parts of the Pays d'Auge. Further east, extending through Artois into Flanders, and criss-crossed by the 'Flemish graben' (rifts), the older rocks are overlaid with a thick layer of chalk deposited by the sea about 200 million years ago. Above the chalk is a thinner covering of loam, scattered throughout which is the flint (silex) so characteristic of Normandy. Along the coast, faults in the chalk give rise to the *falaises*, sheer cliffs often more than 150 m high; similar faults inland form the lines of the river valleys. It is only in the Ardennes, further east still, that the hills are once again composed of slate and older rocks.

Different districts — local variety

As you drive through northern France and Normandy you are crossing a whole network of smaller sub-regions, some of which, like the Pays d'Auge, take their names from the geology (*auge* means a trough or valley), others, like the *Bocage*, from the vegetation (*bocage* means scrub or thicket). Some are relics of old administrative divisions predating the French Revolution and the present-day regions (Picardy, Artois), others of the Napoleonic system of departments (Calvados). These names do more than create variety on the map; they mark regional peculiarities which gladden the heart of locals and visitors alike. Keen-eyed observers will discover revealing differences in the local landscapes, in the methods of cultivation and division of fields, in animal husbandry and in the kinds of habitation.

The tides

Life on the northern coasts is regulated by the tides *(marées)*, the effects of periodic disturbance of the earth's gravitational field caused primarily by the moon. The largest tidal ranges in Europe (up to 15 m) are recorded around the Cotentin peninsula, and especially at Mont-St-Michel where sometimes the tide recedes up to 15 km at low water, only to return on the flood at terrific speed, which makes the bay particularly dangerous. The proximity to the Atlantic Ocean, the nature of the coast, depth of water and strength of current make for local tidal anomalies almost everywhere, in addition to which there are the variations between spring and neap tides produced by the different phases of the moon. It is not only navigation and fishing that are dependent on the tides; watersports and beach life are equally affected. Official tide tables *(horaires des marées)* are displayed in hotels as well as on the beaches. As a rough rule of thumb, about twelve and a half hours elapse between each high water (and each low water).

The English Channel

The English Channel (*la Manche*) is 350 miles long. From being 120 ft deep at its eastern end it drops away to a depth of 360 ft in the west. On the French side (more than half of which is formed by the coasts of Normandy and the departments adjoining it to the north-east) exceptionally strong tides prevail. The tidal difference between west and east is about seven hours. Of the water entering the Channel from the Atlantic, reaching its maximum rate of flow at Cherbourg, approximately 22% continues into the North Sea and from there back into the ocean. The Channel is 150 miles wide between the Gulf of St-Malo (Brittany) and Lyme Bay (England), narrowing to only 24 miles at the Straits of Dover (in French *Pas de Calais*). As early as 1802, at the instigation of Napoleon, the French engineer Mathieu drew up the first ever plans for the construction of a tunnel to link the two coasts. Queen Victoria and Winston Churchill also considered such a project, and the idea was revived again in 1956 following the Suez crisis. In 1986 France and the UK finally signed the contract for the so-called Eurotunnel. A special company was formed, financed by private share capital, to drive the tunnel 130 ft beneath the seabed. Construction teams working from both sides finally made contact with each other in November 1990. Designed to provide a rail link only, the 31-mile-long double tunnel running between Sangatte (near Calais) and Ashford (near Folkestone) is scheduled to open in 1993.

The Channel in history

Waterways divide, but they also form links. Today's idea of the English Channel as a partition separating France from the British Isles is actually a very one-sided view of things. To document the full history of all its crossings would involve adding to the many thousands of naval and merchant vessels not only little boats of animal hide carrying the early missionaries, and many another small craft ferrying fugitives, but also numbers of festively adorned wedding barges; all of these have sailed over this waterway.

Neither Christians nor heathens ever considered the English Channel a hindrance to their ambitions. From the 6th c. onwards monks from Ireland and Scotland joyfully crossed it to preach the gospels on the Continent; to experienced Viking voyagers setting off on raids over the water the passage must have seemed no more than a step. The Anglo-Saxon kings and their entourages in turn fled from the Vikings to Normandy and Flanders. In 1064 Harold (shortly to become king of England) was supposedly shipwrecked in the Channel and rescued by vassals of his rival William of Normandy, only to be killed two years later at the Battle of Hastings, the first action in the Norman invasion and conquest of England in 1066.

In the Norman domains under William's descendants, and in Henry II's much larger realm which extended from Scotland to the Pyrenees in the late twelfth century, the Channel must have served to connect rather than divide. During the Hundred Years War between France and England (1339–1453), however, the cross-Channel traffic became threatening and one-way, bringing repeated English incursions into France. Then in 1588 the inhabitants of the Channel coast witnessed the greatest sea battle of the early modern period when the English fleet defeated the Spanish Armada off Calais.

The Channel offered a safe landfall to anyone who was forced to flee his own country. In the 17th c. it was the English aristocracy in particular who sought refuge, the Stuarts amongst them – including James II who, after the landing of his brother-in-law William of Orange in 1689, went into exile in France. Following the French Revolution the trend was reversed. It is true that Napoleon Bonaparte never set foot on English shores, but after him there was scarcely a ruler of France who did not contrive somehow to arrive incognito on English soil – Louis XVIII before he succeeded Napoleon in 1814, his brother Charles X, forced to abdicate in 1830, and Napoleon III who died in exile in England in 1873. Queen Victoria (1837–1901) in contrast crossed the Channel only for purposes of State, or for pleasure.

Essential details in brief

Normandy

Normandy is divided into five departments: Seine-Maritime and Eure which form Upper Normandy (Haute Normandie), and Calvados, Orne and Manche forming Lower Normandy (Basse Normandie). Rouen is the chief city of the whole of Normandy.

Population: 2.8 million; *population density:* 100 per sq km, 77 per sq km in Basse Normandie, 134 per sq km in Haute Normandie.

Area: 29,841 sq km; *coastline:* 600 km.

Longest rivers: Seine, Risle, Orne and Vire.

Ports: Le Havre, France's largest port after Marseilles; Rouen, the third largest French river port and France's fifth largest port; Cherbourg, a naval and commercial port.

Agriculture: 11.5% of the working population are engaged in agriculture (the average for France as a whole is 8.2%). Most important products: meat, milk and butter (Normandy supplies more than a quarter of France's total output of these products) as well as cheese, Calvados, vegetables, wheat, sugar-beet and fruit; about 6 million head of cattle of which 1 million are dairy cows. Horse-breeding is also an important source of income.

Industry: food products, timber and smaller-scale light industries such as glass, copperwork, textiles, electrical products, chemicals and pharmaceuticals; ship-building (particularly in Cherbourg). Oil refineries at the large ports account for 35% of French capacity. La Hague (Cotentin) has the largest nuclear reprocessing plant in Europe.

Nord-Pas-de-Calais

This region, consisting of the two separate departments of Nord and Pas-de-Calais, takes in the most westerly parts of the former counties of Flanders (Flandre) and Hainaut (both now mainly Belgian) as well as the old county of Artois and the Boulonnais region.

Population: 3.9 million; the population density of 316 per sq km is three times that of the rest of France.

Area: 12,439 sq km; *coastline:* 145 km.

Longest rivers: Scheldt, Lys, Sambre and Oise.

Ports: Dunkirk (Dunkerque), third largest commercial port in France; Calais, the largest passenger port on the European mainland; Boulogne, France's largest fishing port.

Industry: the centre of the French textile industry, producing one third of the country's cotton, 95% of its wool and almost all its linen; also coal, non-ferrous metal and steel production; chemical, petrochemical and food industries (wheat, chicory and fish).

Phases of history

Celts and Romans

The first settlers, whose presence in Normandy can be traced back to around 3600 BC, came from the Danube region; they were followed 2,000 years later by the Celts. In 56 BC the Romans reached the Channel coast in their conquest of northern Gaul, creating two provinces, Lugdunensis in the west and Belgica in the east, which were later to become Normandy. As early as AD 260 the first evidence of Christianity can be traced around Rouen, then known as Rotumagos. By the 4th c. there is mention of churches and of bishoprics in Sées, Evreux and Avranches.

The Frankish empire

The Franks, who since AD 350 had lived in peaceful co-existence with the Romans, extended their lands westward from the Somme to the area north of the Seine. Here they established an independent kingdom under Childeric. Following his son Clovis's victory over Syagrius, 'last of the Roman kings', at Soissons in 486, this Merovingian kingdom grew into one of the main centres of power in the Frankish empire. After partition of the empire, the former Roman lands in the west between the Scheldt and the Loire were renamed Neustria, and later Francia.

From the beginning of the 6th c. onwards Christianity became ever more widely disseminated. Monks played an important part in this process and the 7th c. saw the founding of many monasteries. Along the banks of the Seine, three great saints were particularly instrumental in this: Ouen, Bishop of Rouen, Wandrille who founded Fontenelle (subsequently to be named after him; see page 65), and Philibert who founded Jumièges. The monasteries of Fécamp, St-Céneri and Mont-St-Michel (708) were established soon afterwards.

The Vikings

With the death of Charlemagne (814) the unity of the vast Frankish empire crumbled. The ensuing state of weakness was exploited to the full by the Vikings on their raids (see page 16). King Charles the Simple's treaty with the Viking Rollo in 911 turned the raiders into defenders, but also into increasingly powerful vassals of a duchy which in time came to bear proudly the name of its conquerors, the Norsemen, or Normans. Under Rollo's five successors – the Norman dukes whose courts were in Rouen and Fécamp – Normandy, long oppressed, flourished economically and culturally. In a veritable fever of reconstruction the ravaged monasteries and cathedrals were rebuilt, and new ones were established, in which great scholars and theologians like Lanfranc, St Anselm of Canterbury and William of Volpiano worked. To counter growing resistance from the nobility the dukes, and in particular William the Bastard following the Battle of Val-ès-Dunes and the Peace of Caen (1047), established an unusually strong form of centralised government. After the 13th c. this became the model for the French kingdom, to which Normandy itself eventually succumbed.

William the Conqueror and his successors

The unresolved question of succession following the death of the last Anglo-Saxon king, the childless Edward the Confessor, gave William the Bastard, as a blood relative, reason to invade England in 1066 with a fleet and 50,000 men. On October 14th at the Battle of Hastings he defeated his rival Harold, who had been hastily crowned king that same year. From then onwards William was known by a new title, 'the Conqueror'. Though he was crowned king on Christmas Day, it was a further five years before his conquest of England was finally completed. He and his six successors then ruled over the combined kingdom of England and duchy of Normandy, as dangerously powerful vassals of the French king.

Normandy becomes French

In 1199 with the death of Henry II's son Richard I (the Lionheart), the tide of events turned in favour of France. Appointed regent while his brother Richard was imprisoned in Germany, the weak John Lackland had been forced by the French king, Philippe II, to renounce all claim to Upper Normandy. Although Richard successfully regained the lost possessions after his release, when John succeeded to the throne he was unable to hold on to Normandy, being plagued at home in England by rebellious nobles. Following the capture of the mighty fortress of Gaillard and the surrender of Rouen in 1204, the region again fell into Philippe's hands. In 1214 John, who by then had formed an alliance with the German emperor, was finally defeated at the Battle of Bouvines. After this success the French king adopted the title of Philippe Auguste ('Augustus').

And so from a political point of view Normandy became French. Romano-French culture, on the other hand, had long been at home here, ineradicably implanted to the extent even of the language which the Normans exported to England. In the centuries which followed, Normandy was to exercise an important influence on the cultural development of France. This influence was very evident in the period of High Gothic (see page 17), as well as during the Renaissance.

Such importance did the French kings attach to their new possessions that in 1315 they set down their rights in the 'Norman Charter', at the same time instituting an assembly known as the 'Echiquier'. The Charter was reaffirmed repeatedly up to 1485. From 1333 onwards there were even dukes of Normandy once again, the first being Jean le Bon (John the Good), created duke by his father Philippe VI. The last duke, Charles (brother of King Louis XI), having been deprived of office, was forced in 1469 to watch as the ducal signet-ring was ceremonially shattered by the King's lieutenant-general in the Hall of the Echiquier in Rouen; this marked the irreversible integration of Normandy into the French empire following the Hundred Years War.

The Hundred Years War

This bloody war was brought about by the end of the Capetian dynasty and the claim by marriage of the Anglo-Norman kings to the French throne. Parts of Normandy, the main scene of the fighting, were devastated. Being under English rule again from 1415 until about 1440 served also to revive Norman aspirations for independence from France. Strengthened however by victory over the English – a victory set in train by Joan of Arc – the French kings of the House of Valois were eventually able to re-establish their authority. Normandy was from then on ruled by a governor. In 1499 the Echiquier was dissolved, being replaced for a short period by a court of law before a regional parliament was introduced in 1515.

Emigration and internal conflict

In the 16th and 17th c. the Normans were once more called upon to practise their ancient skills as navigators, not least to keep open the new Atlantic trade routes over which the Portuguese held sway. Ships set sail from Dieppe, Honfleur and Le Havre (founded by François I in 1517), reaching out for Brazil, New York, Florida and 'La Nouvelle France' where, from the establishing of Quebec in 1608, the new colony of Canada had been settled almost entirely by farmers from Normandy.

There were certainly plenty of reasons for emigrating, among them the plague. But it was above all the Wars of Religion which caused the Huguenots in particular to flee the country. Even today many Normandy churches bear the marks of destruction wrought by religious zealots. Eventually Henri IV gained two decisive victories over the Catholic League, at Arques in 1589 and at Ivry in 1590 (the towns still have 'la-Bataille' – battle – appended to their names). Continuing rebellion among the aristocracy – supported in part by English Protestants – prompted Henri to impose government by three regional administrators, in Rouen, Caen and Alençon, as well as to dismantle many of the old fortifications. The absolutism of his grandson Louis XIV, which forced the aristocracy to take up residence at Court, finally completed the centralisation of power. It was a policy of enlightened state control, orchestrated by the King's minister Colbert, which successfully revived the regional economy following the renewed expulsion of the Huguenots, who until then had been major contributors to it.

It was left to Louis XVI to indulge in one final evocation of the past, when the heir to the throne was made duke of Normandy in 1775.

France acquires its north-eastern boundary

In the course of the extended hostilities between Spain and France the Spanish part of the Netherlands came increasingly under French control. The Treaty of the Pyrenees (1659) secured for France parts of Flanders and the county of Hainaut, together with the county of Artois. Having married the Spanish princess Maria-Theresa, Louis XIV later laid claim to the whole of the Spanish Netherlands, embarking upon the so-called War of Devolution. Lille passed to France in 1668, and in 1679 under the Treaty of Nijmwegen Spain was forced to give up further territory in west Flanders, including Cambrai. This has remained France's definitive north-eastern border ever since the Congress of Vienna in 1815, prior to which the frontier had been pushed east as far as the Elbe in the Revolutionary and Napoleonic Wars.

The French Revolution and the 19th century

The Revolution was at first greeted with enthusiasm in Normandy and the north – Robespierre was actually born in Arras. Later, however, Caen became the centre of opposition by the moderate Girondins. An army was formed to challenge the radical Jacobins and dispatched to Paris, but it was halted and defeated at Vernon. In 1793 Charlotte Corday, who came from a village in Normandy south of Lisieux, also failed in her attempt to change the course of events, despite murdering the Jacobin Marat.

With Louis XIV's wars the North Sea coast of France had once again been turned into the English 'front', newly fortified with defenceworks constructed by the famous architect Sébastien Vauban. The dream of successive French rulers to make a victorious landing on English shores foundered repeatedly on the Channel coast. In

1692 a French invasion fleet had been destroyed by the English at La Hougue on the Cotentin peninsula. In 1803 Napoleon, with similar intent, gathered together a large military and naval force in Boulogne, but he abandoned his invasion plans two years later to engage in a campaign against Austria. In 1840 things were reversed when Napoleon III arrived at Boulogne from England to mount an unsuccessful surprise attack against the Citizen King, Louis Philippe – for which Napoleon paid with six years' imprisonment in the fortress at Ham on the Somme.

As a direct result of the 'Continental System' (the blockade imposed by Napoleon I in 1806 to prevent British trade with the Continent) industry and sugar-beet cultivation prospered in Normandy, especially along the Seine and in association with the developing Channel ports. Prosperity increased also in Nord and Pas-de-Calais where the iron and non-ferrous metal industries were established to exploit the deposits of ore and coal.

On the one hand industry – on the other bathing resorts! In 1806 an astonished crowd was present in Dieppe to see a certain Madame de Boignes take her very first dip in the sea. She initiated a fashion which led to the thriving 19th c. seaside holiday industry, whose growth was accelerated still further by the new railway line from Paris to Rouen (opened in 1843 and later extended to Lillebonne and Le Havre). The north and Normandy again became a battleground during the Franco-Prussian War of 1870–71 which, among other things, led to the downfall of Napoleon III and the declaration of the Third Republic. The German army advanced through Belgium, through St-Quentin and Amiens, and into Haute Normandie as far as Rouen, which they occupied in December 1870.

The two World Wars

In the First World War Normandy was spared. Not so the region to the north-east, however. The front ran from Bruges through Flanders, Artois and Picardy to the Somme. Marshal Foch's headquarters were at Cassel, near St-Omer. From here in 1914–15 the Marshal set out for the battlefields of Flanders and the Yser. It was also from here that in 1918, as commander-in-chief of the Allied forces, he forced the Germans into accepting unconditional surrender following heavy fighting on the Marne and in Picardy.

The Second World War began for France on May 10th 1940, when the German Wehrmacht once again invaded, along a front running from Dunkirk to the Ardennes and the Somme. They reached Paris on June 14th, imposing unconditional surrender just as Marshal Foch had done in the forest of Compiègne in 1918. The north of France was separated from the rest of the country. It became an occupied area in which the Germans erected the 'Atlantic Wall' against the British – some 10,000 concrete structures ranging from dug-out shelters to huge bunkers built by prisoners of war. Many of these defences have survived, almost certainly the largest being at Eperlecques, near St-Omer. It stood 22 m high and was intended as the launch site for the destruction of London. Serving now as museums, large and small, the bunkers, like thousands of war graves in cemeteries behind the coast, are grim reminders of the 1944 Normandy Landings in which the Allied troops stormed 'Fortress Europe'. This massive sea- and airborne operation, code-named 'Overlord', with General Eisenhower in command, had been conceived at a meeting of the Allies in Quebec the previous year.

Remains of the Allies' prefabricated harbour, Gold Beach

While the bunkers (which are also found on the Channel Islands) mostly survived the battles, the same cannot be said of many of the towns and villages of Normandy which, on top of the destruction wrought by the German forces after D-Day – the so-called 'Longest Day' – were completely reduced to rubble and ashes by Allied bombing. Parts of the Normandy coast between the Cotentin peninsula and the mouth of the Orne are still called by the code names used for the Allied landings on the night of June 5th/6th 1944. The Utah and Omaha beaches in the western sector were the target for American troops while, to the east of Arromanches – around which the assault centred – Gold, Juno and Sword beaches were seized by British and Canadian troops. Starting on June 7th a huge harbour was created within a week, constructed from concrete caissons prefabricated in England. Its capacity was equal to that of Le Havre at the time.

The whole operation ended on August 21st 1944 with the Battle of Falaise. The German forces, assembled for a counter-offensive, were encircled in what became known as the Falaise Pocket (*la poche de Falaise*). On August 25th, together with American troops, the Free French army under Charles de Gaulle entered Paris.

From Norsemen to Normans

Vikings, Varangians and Norsemen: the names may be different but they conjure up a single image – of the early inhabitants of Scandinavia seeking out new shores across the sea. The Norwegian Vikings reached northern England, Scotland, Ireland, Iceland, Greenland and North America. On their expeditions to Byzantium and on their homeward journeys, the Swedish Vikings, the 'Rus' (Slav for rowers), settled the heartland of present-day Russia, the area around Kiev and Novgorod. Danes and Norwegians voyaged to the south of England and by way of Friesland along the North Sea coast to the Frankish empire, on to Spain, then Italy and as far as Antioch. Finding nothing to plunder in Iceland and Greenland, the Vikings settled them instead, and from there set off on further voyages of discovery to Vinland (America). The Varangians – traders as well as warriors – dealt in furs, silver and slaves, all procured on raiding expeditions which at times involved little more than kidnap and extortion. In Byzantium they early turned themselves into allies of the Emperor, ensuring their own safety by serving as imperial bodyguards. As merchants there they assiduously cultivated their own interests.

When in 793 the Vikings attacked the monastery at Lindisfarne, lighting the first terrible flame in what turned out to be 120 years of looting and pillage, they were doing no more than living up to their name (*vikingr* means pirate or robber). At first they chose to attack monasteries which, being unfortified, were at their mercy whilst also holding out the promise of food, treasure, and human beings – an important factor for these heathen freebooters who made a practice of trading in slaves. The cry of 'God protect us from the Norsemen' would go up as the swift and easily manoeuvred Viking ships came in sight off the coast with their red sails, though usually under oars as well. The elaborately carved figureheads were pointed towards the river mouths, into which the boats could pass without difficulty on account of their shallow draught. To the terrifying sound of horns and armed with swords, axes, spears and arrows (later also astride armoured horses which they brought with them in their ships), the raiders would fall on those unfortunates who had time neither to flee nor to save the relics of the Christian saints. The Vikings robbed, pillaged and butchered before taking the survivors, especially the women, away with them as slaves. In time they came to accept the Danegeld (a form of protection money) in return for refraining from threatened raids, or – well informed on local affairs – they allowed themselves to be enlisted by rival feudal lords, usually to wage their wars for them but sometimes also to protect them against the next wave of Viking raiders.

Today, however, the Norsemen or 'Normanni' are also admired as knights and rulers. In 911 the West Frankish king Charles the Simple managed to make a vassal out of Rollo, one of the leaders of a Viking army which had ravaged Rouen and Paris. The following year Rollo accepted Christianity and Charles granted him first the devastated bishoprics of Rouen, Evreux, and Lisieux, and later the whole of Normandy. Rollo proclaimed himself duke of Normandy, married the King's daughter, restored its property to the Church and secured the safety of the region, which until the 11th c. was to be threatened repeatedly by the advancing Vikings.

In a short time the picture had further changed. The Normans with their great adaptability and organisational skill became wielders of State and feudal power, responsible for spreading Christianity and reforming the churches and monasteries.

By the third generation these erstwhile foreigners could no longer speak Danish. Rollo's grandson Richard had to learn it specially in Bayeux, although, as the tapestry demonstrates, other customs and skills from the old homeland were preserved for a long time afterwards.

The Normans remained a proud and restless people, however. Those in political disfavour, or younger sons without inheritance, set out over the seas as their forefathers had done, in search of fresh shores. By 999 they had secured themselves a niche as knights to the Lombard and Byzantine rulers of southern Italy. Less than a century later, by 1091, the whole of southern Italy, together with Sicily which had been wrested from the Saracens, was under Norman rule. The twelve sons of the Hauteville family from the Cotentin peninsula are almost legendary. One, Robert Guiscard, took up arms against both the German and the Byzantine emperors, coincidentally encountering the Varangian guard from Byzantium. When in 1095 the Pope appealed for people to join the first Crusade against the Mussulmans it was the Normans of England, France and Italy who provided the greatest armies of knights. In one final 'Viking incursion' they took Antioch. No more dragon ships were to come from Scandinavia. The spread of Christianity and the increasing power of the kings in the nation-states of Norway, Sweden and Denmark spelled the end of the Viking period.

Art and architecture

Churches and monasteries

Normandy has outstanding churches representing every stylistic phase, from the Middle Ages in particular, but also from the Renaissance and the classical period (as the Baroque era is called in France, its motifs and guiding principles differing from those of Italian Baroque and its derivatives). In the Romanesque period Norman architecture developed with an independence unmatched elsewhere, and in St-Etienne in Caen and the abbey churches of St-Martin-de-Boscherville, Lessay and Jumièges Normandy possesses some of the most perfect examples. Early and Late Gothic found their purest expression in the region to the east of Normandy, in the cathedrals of Amiens, Laon and Beauvais. The Romanesque churches of Normandy are distinguished by the purity of their proportions, the boldness of their construction and the daring of their dimensions. The twin-towered façades are horizontally articulated, giving the overall effect of a Latin H. They show too a surprising degree of variation, and a sureness of touch in the arrangement of windows and decoration. The master builders who erected these churches from the late 11th c. onwards were Benedictine monks. Normandy Gothic — with which Romanesque elements were often fused as can be seen, for example, in Bayeux — acquired its distinctive character in the 13th c. At Coutances and Rouen, for instance, the delight of the builders in original detail and constructional refinements is evident throughout.

Late Gothic in France is also known as *le style flamboyant*. Notre-Dame in Alençon is a fine example, but perfect illustrations of this late, richly decorated style can also be found in quite modest places, like Caudebec-en-Caux where the church is likewise dedicated to Notre-Dame.

Castles, châteaux and manor houses

Normandy has innumerable examples of these. They sometimes follow one another in such quick succession that you cannot help wondering how much land each incumbent could have possessed.

There are countless Renaissance châteaux, some of them not even classified as historic monuments *(monuments classés)*. They often stand on the sites of Early Norman timber houses which were built on artificial mounds. The feudal architecture of the Middle Ages reflects the fact that a castle could be built only with the permission of the duke. In giving it he would aim to secure his own borders and would retain the right to quarter his troops there. The castle at Gisors and that of Robert le Diable on the Seine are among the earliest examples. Château Gaillard and the castles at Etelan and Falaise date from the Gothic period.

In the later châteaux and manor houses *(manoirs)*, whose architects were less preoccupied with defence, regional styles developed, leading to such graceful creations as the small moated châteaux of Coupesarte — half-timbered in the Norman style — and Victot-Pontfol, built in brick. Fontaine-Henry and Tourlaville are important examples of Renaissance châteaux, while 17th c. classical architecture can be seen at its most typical in the châteaux of Champ-de-Bataille and Beaumesnil. Rouen boasts the largest number of medieval and Renaissance buildings, both secular and sacred; they have been wonderfully resurrected out of the devastation of the Second World War.

The dovecot — *le colombier*

Dovecots, already known from Roman times, had a special significance in Normandy in the Middle Ages; no one apart from the owners of feudal estates was allowed to keep an unlimited number of the birds, which it was forbidden to hunt. Token of this right (a right abolished only after the French Revolution) was the free-standing dovecot *(colombier à pied)*. The manner in which large stones, bricks, flint and wood are incorporated into the walls gives a distinctive appearance to the dovecots of the different regions. The coats of arms of their former owners are sometimes still to be seen over the entrances of these dual-purpose buildings (domestic animals below, doves above, separated by a wooden floor), and the curved roofs are often crowned by a lead finial, not infrequently finished in the shape of a dove.

Coupesarte — moated château

Right: View of the Seine Valley from Château Gaillard

Normandy and the great painters

In the first half of the 19th c. the French Romantic painters (like their German and English counterparts, some nice distinctions notwithstanding) began to discover nature, but it was not until after 1860 that Impressionism, for many the culmination of this discovery, came into being. Normandy had an important part to play at the very outset. Born in Honfleur, Eugène Boudin did much of his painting of his native coasts in the open air, and filled the young Claude Monet with enthusiasm for this approach. Up to the time of the Franco-Prussian War, Normandy, particularly its coast and the Seine, was a favourite place for the Impressionists, although only Monet remained unswervingly loyal to it, finally settling in Giverny.

The Pointillists who arrived next on the scene created the effects of light and colour in their compositions by means of the juxtaposition of tiny dots. They also took inspiration from Normandy, its sky and its sea, as too did the Fauves in whose paintings strong, even violent, colouring assumes greater importance than any object. Marquet, Friesz and van Dongen found here in Normandy the milieu they needed for their work. Raoul Dufy, one of the most charming decorative painters of the century, came from Le Havre. The museum there has excellent examples of his work, together with an exquisite collection of paintings by Boudin. The galleries in Rouen and Lille are well endowed with Impressionist paintings, while in Giverny Monet's flower garden and lily pond are as well tended today as during the painter's lifetime — instead of the paintings, the living subjects!

Rouen pottery

One of the earliest of all large pottery factories was operating in Rouen from 1644 onwards. Rouen faience came to be held in high esteem after December 3rd 1689 when, bled by the cost of his various wars, the Sun King, Louis XIV, created a fashion by having his silver melted down and replaced with glazed pottery. Ceramics having become acceptable at Court, Rouen was in vogue. The factory no longer followed the leads provided by Faenza or Delft, but evolved its own decorative style, the *décor rayonné*, in which *broderies* (lace- or embroidery-like patterns) or *lambrequins* (pendant-like designs) radiate around a central point. Even with much more space it would be impossible to do justice to the variety of ceramic work produced in Rouen, its early 18th c. tile-topped tables, its imitations of Chinese porcelain, its distinctive colouring, especially the rust-red but also the honey-yellow and the blue. In 1722 there were eleven factories in Rouen. By 1783 the number had risen to eighteen, a sure sign that here as elsewhere pottery was already being mass-produced. By around 1700 northern France — Lille and St-Omer included — had become one of the country's main areas of pottery production, its output imitated by Strasbourg as well as by Ansbach. In the *Musée de la Céramique* in Rouen it is possible not only to follow the development of the local industry but also to compare it with equivalent products from other factories and other countries as far away as China; this provides a fascinating insight into a craft whose best examples from Rouen are as precious as the finest silver.

✕ Food and drink

from Dunkirk to Brittany one of the nicest things about the food in northern France is that it is 'natural', the produce of sea and pasture. The sea offers a choice between *otte de mer* (a fish of the cod family), sole and John Dory, or, for something a little more modest but nutritious and good value, between mackerel and ray – always assuming, that is, that you don't prefer scallops, crab, shrimps and oysters. Herds of cows grazing on the lush pastures, which are an integral part of the pleasant rural scenery, provide the finest-quality milk, cream, butter and cheese. And in a countryside devoid of vines the apple-trees ensure that you do not have to forgo delicious drinks. There is Calvados and there is cider, high and not so high in alcohol content. Normandy cuisine is not particularly refined, but it is nourishing and portions are generous. It is certainly not sparing of cream or flour, and the favourite side-dish is French fries, which in Nord, served with mussels, make a popular main meal, *moules et frites*. Lille, where those two foods are even honoured with their own festival, has the best of Nord's restaurants, to which the *Guide Michelin* has awarded more than one star – though not for *moules et frites*!

Les tripes (tripe) is another famous northern speciality and indeed is in demand all over France when served *à la mode de Caen*, though it may not be to everyone's liking. The *andouillette* from Nord, called *andouille* in some places, is a sausage filled either with *tripes* or with butchers' scraps, especially chitterling. The offal is scraped, washed, rinsed, cooked, and then rinsed yet again. According to people with a taste for it, this delicacy deserves to be much more widely appreciated than it is.

Another recipe which illustrates the uncomplicated, country style of Normandy cooking is its famous *sauce normande*, a cream sauce which can be served with virtually anything – fish or poultry, meat or vegetables.

Sadly, however, you would seldom guess when eating out in one of the northern departments that some of the best and most tender vegetables are grown in Artois and Picardy. The splendid cauliflowers from St-Omer and carrots from St-Valery are nowadays hardly ever served. Convenience foods have long since taken over in the cheaper establishments and even in the gourmet restaurants recommended by the *Guide Michelin*, the *Bottin Gourmand* and the *Gault Millau*. Their assessments seem to be based more on the distinctive blend of ingredients than on the quality of the vegetables themselves. The region's famous soups – including pumpkin, frog, tripe and beer soups – are likewise served only rarely.

Picardy has a whole range of distinctive dishes, often not exactly light, which you find served in the many restaurants with the word 'Picard' or 'Picardie' on their signs. *Flamiche picarde*, for instance, is a sort of leek pudding made with eggs and cream, while *rissoles* are puff-pastry envelopes with deep-fried fish or meat, again with a cream sauce. Amiens duck pie is delicious and is fairly widely available. On the other hand, even though there are a number of good-quality cheeses from the north-east they are not nearly as well known as the Normandy cheeses *Livarot*, *Pont-l'Evêque* and the relative newcomer *Camembert*, which is not 200 years old, while the praises of the other two have been sung ever since the Middle Ages.

Canard à la rouennaise (Rouen duckling – perhaps Normandy's most celebrated poultry recipe) is no less ancient. The duck is part roasted and then part boned; the juices are squeezed from it and used to baste it before it is finally cooked through in

Specialities of northern France

a hot oven. Normandy poultry is of the best quality, and the beef is as good as that from Charolais.

In Brittany and Normandy *crêpes* – paper-thin pancakes brought to the table direct from the hot griddle – are served sweet or savoury, with every possible filling. Crêpes, though, are just a snack, and to make a full meal of them at a *crêperie* would be expensive.

Sandwich and *snack* are light meals available in many bars, and are good value for money. Throughout France a *sandwich* means a large piece of crusty *baguette* generously filled and garnished. *Croque monsieur* and *croque madame* are varieties of toasted sandwich.

Oysters are sold on the coast at stalls in front of the large food markets, and cost next to nothing. *Moules* and *huîtres farcies* – mussels and oysters sprinkled with butter, cream or cheese and put under the grill for a few minutes – are absolutely elicious. As for the *plateau de fruits de mer* found on menus near the coast, whether or not you tackle it depends very much on your stamina and sense of adventure. Often served as a portion for two, the *plateau* comes with crab and sea-snails as well as oysters and prawns. It takes quite a bit of eating, and a willingness to try new things.

Pommes à la normande

'Normandy potato' is a typical Normandy recipe made with leeks and cream, and not over-heavy. It is suitable as a snack on its own, or as an accompaniment to many different dishes.

For four to five persons: 750 g raw, peeled and sliced potatoes; three leeks cut in rings (up to the light-green tops); one onion also cut in rings; 150 g cubed lean bacon; 1.5 dl fresh cream; ½ l bouillon; 80 g butter; salt, white pepper and parsley. Cooking time thirty minutes.

Fry the onion, bacon and leeks in butter until a pale golden brown, add the potatoes and then season. Cover with the bouillon and leave till all ingredients are cooked. Remove from the heat, stir in the fresh cream, reheat for a minute or two and sprinkle with parsley before serving.

Cider (apple-juice of varying degrees of sparkle, with a 3% to 4% alcohol content) is a refreshing and tasty drink. There are many varieties ranging roughly from dry *(sec or brut)* to medium-dry *(demi-sec)* and sweet *(doux)*. *Calvados*, an apple schnapps with a good 40% to 50% alcohol content, is distilled from cider. *Appellation d'origine* on the label guarantees the genuineness of its geographical origin. The aroma and colour depend on the way in which it is laid down, and for how long. It is drunk at almost every opportunity!

Right: Normandy is famous for its cheeses

Below: Crab-fishermen

Hints for your holiday

Getting to know the whole of the north of France, Normandy included, would take a long time. As far as the very north is concerned, many of those who simply drive through it on the way to Normandy never really become acquainted with it. But you should definitely stop off for a while and look around. Keen eyes and curiosity are well rewarded here where the French border-country merges into Belgium. Historically the two belong together, but history has also arbitrarily separated them.

Few holidaymakers think of the north coast of France as a place for enjoying a beach holiday. After all, despite the mildness of the climate influenced by the Gulf Stream this area can offer no guarantee of day-long sunbathing. The summers are short, the waters of the Channel become only moderately warm, the weather is changeable, and there is also the wind. But this takes no account at all of how exciting it can be to follow the tides as they uncover the underwater world of the beach. Oysters — fruit of the tide's ebb and flow — don't get fat here; they stay small, firm and fresh.

Behind the coast extend woods, meadows and vast fields, bounded on the horizon by the silhouettes of trees straining inland away from the onshore wind. Cathedrals, churches, châteaux, half-timbered and manor houses, and castles built along the Seine are all there to be visited *en route*. And every now and then you will catch a glimpse of a lonely farmstead, encircled by its earth mounds on which, for a thousand years, trees have been planted to form a natural boundary.

Beauvais Cathedral

Where to go and what to see
Picardy, Nord and Pas-de-Calais

Except on the coast there are very few holiday areas in this varied part of north-east France, between Normandy and Belgium, whose natural and man-made sub-divisions never quite seem to coincide. Even so, it is well worth visiting some of the lovely towns and other sights in the region, even if only to leave the motorway for a while and relax. The most important of the cathedrals are to be found in the south, between Laon and Beauvais (north of Reims and Paris respectively) and up as far as Amiens. This area is described first of all. Then the motorway routes to Dunkirk and Calais are considered, together with several detours. Finally this section of the book deals with some of the sights and natural features of the coast and its hinterland from the Belgian frontier to Haute Normandie.

The southern cathedral cities and their environs

Laon Pop. 29,000
Administrative centre of the Aisne department
Driving some 50 km north-west from Reims on the motorway brings you to Laon, one-time Carolingian capital, strikingly situated on a long ridge standing out above the surrounding plain. The two districts crowning the hilltop, the *Cité* around the cathedral and *Le Bourg* around the church of St-Martin, form either end of the *haute ville* (upper town), which repays some time just walking through it and along the ramparts. The architectural unity of the streets, the Renaissance and 17th c.

mansions, the old town gates, the *museum* with its archaeological collections, Greek vases and art gallery, and finally the churches, above all the cathedral, make Laon a jewel among the towns of northern France.

 Around the cathedral

The façade of the cathedral of *Notre-Dame* is a marvellous piece of Early Gothic architecture with its 56-m-high, richly articulated towers, its galleries, and its projecting entrances with their magnificent figures, some of which have been partially restored. Begun in the late 12th c. the building was completed in 1235, a perfect example of the merging of the Late Romanesque spirit with the new Gothic, the latter influence most conspicuously revealed by the crossing-tower. The 110-m-long, 24-m-high nave is particularly interesting on account of the fourfold articulation of its walls. Some 13th c. windows as well as the rose window complete the impression of absolute authenticity, an impression likewise created by the square in front of the cathedral with its old *hôtels* and *palais* (aristocratic mansions).

The *Chapelle des Templiers* close to the museum is an octagonal Romanesque building, while the church of *St-Martin* with its twin-towered façade is a more modest counterpart to the cathedral. Dating from the same period, it is beautifully proportioned and has fine sculptures decorating the tympanum. A magnificent staircase leads up to the *city library*, housed in the 18th c. monastery building attached to the church. The library possesses early manuscripts and incunabula which every year at the end of September are put on show during the Laon Festival's 'Heures médiévales'. A new *rack railway* connects the upper town to the lower.

 Les Chevaliers, tel. 23 23 43 78; *La petite Auberge*, tel. 23 23 02 38.

From Laon drive the 37 km south-west to Soissons.

Soissons Pop. 32,000

Having been the chief settlement of the Celtic Suessioni, and then a Roman garrison, Soissons later played a leading role in the Frankish empire. It became a bishopric as early as the 3rd c.

Opposite: Cathedral of Notre-Dame, Laon

Carved oxen on one of Laon Cathedral's west towers

Soissons Cathedral

 What to see

Built over a period from the 12th to the 14th c., the cathedral of *St-Gervais-et-St-Protais* found itself with only a single tower as a result of the Hundred Years War. Although restoration of the exterior has generally been faithful to the basic design, and has managed to preserve the charm of the rose window and the gallery above it, the façade has nevertheless suffered considerably in the course of time. The *interior*, in consequence, is all the more overwhelming in its effect. The nave and choir, 116 m long, almost 26 m wide and a good 30 m high, are all perfect harmony and symmetry, counterbalanced by the contrasting, wonderfully imaginative design of the transepts. The south transept, divided off in the manner of a choir and apse, leads by way of a covered gallery to a two-storeyed chapel decorated with delightful carvings. The north transept, with its rose window and superb *Adoration of the Shepherds* by Rubens, is also most impressive.

As the result of an imperial decree (and the agreement of the bishop) to the effect that materials should be taken from it to restore the cathedral, the old abbey of *St-Jean-des-Vignes* (St John of the Vineyards, 13th and 14th c.) was left with little more than its twin-towered façade in the early 19th c. All that now remains of the monastery is the refectory, the wine-cellar, and a section of the cloister (endowed with very fine capitals). The church and crypt of the former abbey of *St-Léger* (near the town hall), parts of which date from the 13th c., are also worth seeing.

Compiègne Pop. 43,000

En route to Beauvais you pass through the famous *Forest of Compiègne* with its town of the same name. This is regarded as something of a national shrine by the French. It was here that Joan of Arc was captured by the English, here that the future Louis XVI first met Marie-Antoinette, chosen for political reasons to be his bride, and here that Napoleon III had his favourite residence.

A clearing in the Forest of Compiègne was destined this century to become known the world over. Here in a railway carriage, early on the morning of November 11th 1918, the armistice was signed by Marshal Foch, representing the Entente, and by Matthias Erzberger for the German government under Friedrich Ebert. Twenty-two years later Hitler exacted an almost pathological revenge when, on June 22nd 1940, in the same railway carriage at the self-same spot, he signed another armistice in very different circumstances. The carriage was taken to Berlin as a trophy but disappeared during the War, and has since been replaced by a similar one with authentic furnishings and memorabilia. The place has become a favourite destination for trippers.

The town of Compiègne is charming, a place of pleasant shops, remarkably good restaurants, picturesque corners and — thanks to the presence of the Benjamin Franklin Technical Institute — youthful faces.

 What to see

Despite the many ups and downs in its fortunes the enormous *château* built by Louis XV still harbours some important rooms in suites open to the public. These include the exquisitely appointed games-room in Marie-Antoinette's apartment — never used by the ill-fated Habsburg princess — and a breakfast room dating from 1809 belonging to her niece Marie-Louise. Then there is the oppressive pomp of the Eugénie Room. The huge complex of palace buildings also houses the *Musée du Second Empire* and the *Musée de la Voiture* (motor-car museum) where the late carriages and early cars are particularly interesting.

The *Musée de la Figurine Historique* contains more than 100,000 small fig-

Compiègne town hall — detail

ures made from every conceivable material. It includes some excellent displays of tin figures. The municipal museum, the *Musée Vivenel*, is also worth seeing, with a very varied collection. The Late Gothic belfry of *St-Jacques*, the church which once served the Court, towers over the town. The *town hall* is likewise Late Gothic but bears the all-too-clear imprint of 19th c. restoration.

Ex **The Route des Valois**

The *Route des Valois*, on which there are more than a dozen private castles and châteaux to be visited, criss-crosses an area about 40 km by 70 km from north of Laon to south of Compiègne.

15 km south-east of Compiègne lies *Pierrefonds*, a mighty, late medieval fortress completely restored under Napoleon III by Viollet-le-Duc. *Mongobert*, 12 km further east, is an 18th c. château where a *Wood Museum* occupies three storeys. The château at *Villers-Cotterêts* about 30 km south-east of Compiègne has memorabilia of Alexandre Dumas who was born in the little town. *La Ferté-Milon*, another small town some 10 km to the south, is the birthplace of Racine, France's most famous tragedian. Its *castle* was built in the 15th and 16th c.

16 km south of Compiègne in the little village of *Morienval* (pop. 900) the church of *Notre-Dame* boasts 11th c. stone columns and a 12th c. ambulatory. 8 km away in *Crépy*, former capital of Valois, the château houses two museums, one a *Museum of Christian Art* and the other, unique in its way, the *Musée de l'Archerie* (archery museum).

The Route next turns northwards 40 km to the imposing Gothic ruins of *Ourscamps Abbey*, after which a 5-km detour – an absolute must for all lovers of cathedrals – brings you to Noyon.

Noyon Pop. 14,000

Noyon, founded in the 6th c., was the home town of the Protestant reformer Calvin, born in 1509. It is dominated by the façade and towers of its cathedral, *Notre-Dame*. The more recent of the two towers (14th c.) is among the most beautiful belfries in the north of France. The quadripartite vaulting in the main nave is pure Gothic in the spirit of the Île-de-France; the rounded ends of the transepts in contrast are a rarity, Rhenish in influence. The cathedral library in the adjoining *chapter-house*, an original 16th c. timber building, possesses some early manuscripts and important first editions.

From there it is just a few steps to the *Jean Calvin Museum*, a reconstruction of the house in which the reformer was born. The museum does much to dispel the many misunderstandings surrounding Calvin's achievement.

Beauvais Pop. 54,000

Administrative centre of the Oise department.

In Celtic times this was the main settlement of a tribe called the Bellovaci. It then came under Roman control and

Noyon Cathedral vaulting

was incorporated into the province of Belgica Secunda. Created a bishopric in the 4th c. the city became part of the Frankish empire in the 5th c., and was ravaged by the Norsemen in the 9th c. Later still, in 1589, the Catholic League against the Huguenots was formed here. Before then, however, Beauvais had achieved fame with its Romanesque-Gothic cathedral of *St-Pierre*.

It was in 1225 that the bishop and clergy of Beauvais resolved to build themselves the largest church in Christendom. Primarily as a result of the rivalry between neighbouring towns, pillars and vaulting had already been pushed to previously undreamed-of heights in the cathedrals at Bourges and Chartres. Now all records were to be broken in Beauvais! Work started in 1227, though only the choir was erected. Completed in 1272, this collapsed in 1284 for reasons that are still unexplained. At the time the pillars were thought responsible and they were doubled when rebuilding began after 1337. This ran counter to the original intentions of the design, in which an absolute minimum of structural building was to allow maximum emphasis to be given to the vertical elements. Even so, the 48.2-m-high truncated edifice could still lay claim to being the most daring of cathedral chancels on account of both its technical innovation and the progressive theological thinking behind it.

The Hundred Years War then intervened to prevent any further work on the cathedral and it was not until 1500 that the transepts were added and a new record was created by the construction of a central tower which, at 153 m, was higher than the tower of Strasbourg Cathedral. The Beauvais tower, however, collapsed in 1573, but the chancel remains a marvel of architecture, flooded by the light from its 18-m-high windows, and surrounded by its seven chapels. The Renaissance stained-glass windows in the transepts and the astronomical clock (1865) – modelled on the famous Strasbourg clock – are really no more than pleasing embellishments to this glorious building.

The (post-1500) church of *St-Etienne*, built in the Flamboyant style, also has beautiful Renaissance stained-glass windows, including an especially fine representation of the Tree of Jesse (Christ's genealogy). Since the 17th c. Beauvais has been the site of a branch of the State tapestry manufacturers and can boast a *Galerie Nationale de la Tapisserie* which regularly mounts important exhibitions. Tapestries designed by modern artists are being produced once again in a recently reopened workshop which it is possible to visit. The *Musée Départemental de l'Oise* in the former Bishop's Palace consists mainly of collections of medieval sculpture, French paintings and local pottery.

Au petit Denis, 65 Rue Gambetta, tel. 44 45 05 23; *La Crémaillère*, 1 Rue Gui-Oatin, tel. 44 45 03 13.

Amiens Pop. 136,000
Administrative centre of the Somme department

Amiens, now the provincial capital of Picardy, was originally founded by the Celts. It was the chief town of a Belgic tribe in Gallo-Roman times and was fiercely fought over during the Norman period. It became rich and important later in the Middle Ages, its prosperity being based on a mastery of techniques of dyeing and weaving (wool and silk mixtures). The city was badly damaged in both World Wars, especially the Second. Rebuilt in modern style, Amiens has been a university city since 1964. It

Amiens

is known not only for its cathedral but also for its association with St Martin. It was here in the 4th c. that the Roman officer tore his military cloak in two to clothe a naked beggar. More recently one of Amiens's most famous citizens was the 19th c. writer Jules Verne who came from Nantes.

 What to see

The cathedral of *Notre-Dame* (145 m long) is the biggest Gothic church in France and has the highest nave (the vaulting reaches a height of 42.5 m). It was built between 1220 and 1236, though its towers were erected above the storey with the rose window only in the late 14th c. Viollet-le-Duc, to whom the restoration work of 1849–79 is owed, made one or two not wholly successful alterations to the façade. The exterior, with its heavily articulated west front on which the rose window is positioned at great height, owing to the loftiness of the nave, may not quite stand comparison with the purity of the interior, but with a porch decorated with figures carved in the workshop of Notre-Dame in Paris it is nevertheless one of the great achievements of Gothic sculpture. The left porch depicts St Firmin, patron saint of Picardy, the porch on the right the Virgin Mary, while on either side of the main porch are figures of the apostles, prophets and wise and foolish virgins. In the very centre stands *Le Beau Dieu d'Amiens*, one of the most sublime Christ figures of medieval art. Inside, the *nave* is vast and wonderfully proportioned, its arches being as tall as the two storeys above them, which gives the whole an extraordinary harmony and simplicity. The *choir-stalls* – behind a justly celebrated 18th c. wrought-iron grille in the Late Gothic Flamboyant style – were carved between 1508 and 1519 with about 4,000 small figures embodying countless religious and worldly themes. The ambulatory contains some fine decoration, but the small collection of treasures belonging to the cathedral contains nothing of outstanding interest.

The *Hôtel de Berny*, an elegant Louis XIII building (1634) now the *Musée d'Art Local et de l'Histoire Régionale*, has collections of regional furniture and handicrafts, memorabilia of Amiens's most notable progeny and items of civic history. The resplendent *Musée de Picardie* houses a newly arranged collection of antiquities, some medieval exhibits, works by the Amiens school, and noteworthy French, Italian and Spanish paintings, including some great masters. Definitely worth the short trip by boat in summer is a visit to *les hortillonages*, the so-called 'floating gardens'. Spread over an area of some 300 hectares and enclosed in a tight network of waterways by the encircling arms of the River Somme, the well-tended market gardens can be reached only by boat.

Le Rallye, 24 Rue Otages, tel. 22 91 76 03; *Ibis*, 4 Rue Maréchal-de-Lattre-de-Tassigny, tel. 22 92 57 33; *Coronne*, 64 Rue St-Leu, tel. 22 91 88 57.

Cathedral of Notre-Dame, Amiens

Laon to Dunkirk

Anyone heading for Dunkirk or Calais is most likely to opt for the motorway. An alternative, however, is to take the road north-east towards Belgium, turning off at Maubeuge to join the motorway at Valenciennes. This route is not without its charm – the reality of the northern industrial region is considerably better than its reputation.

Marle, Vervins and Guise. The little town of Marle has a lovely pure Gothic *church* with a graceful Madonna embellishing the west porch. The church of *Notre-Dame* at Vervins – the next stop – has a very fine 16th c. tower. Guise, on the Oise a little to the west, boasts an old *castle*. Extended in the 16th c., its fortifications were modified and strengthened in the 17th c. by Sébastien Vauban.

Avesnes-sur-Helpe. From here you can walk through the *Avesnois* woodland and recreational area as far as the Belgian border. In the closing years of the First World War Avesnes itself was the permanent headquarters of the German generals Hindenburg and Ludendorff. Its *Grande Place* is delightful, and the church of *St-Nicolas* (1534), with its tall bell-tower, is also worth visiting.

Le Cateau-Cambrésis, a short drive west from Avesnes, is an interesting little town with a church, *St-Martin*, built in the Jesuit Baroque style, and a *Grande Place* more reminiscent of Flanders. At the *Musée Henri Matisse* the collection consists largely of early works by this painter, who was born in the town.

Maubeuge, which endured heavy bombing in 1940, has a twenty-eight-bell carillon in the tower of its church, *St-Pierre*, as well as some superb early pieces among the church's treasures. The *Musée Henri Boez* has a collection of considerable local interest.

Bavay, the last worthwhile stop before the motorway, flourished as part of the Roman province of Belgica during the time of Augustus. The actual Roman excavations are likely to be of more interest to the expert than the amateur, who can nevertheless get a vivid picture of Roman life in the *Musée Archéologique*.

The places and sights mentioned next are all accessible from the Laon to Dunkirk motorway which runs via Valenciennes and Lille.

*Exploring
the Avesnois*

La Fère. Some 25 km beyond Laon (see page 26) a short detour takes you into La Fère with its remarkable *Musée Jeanne d'Aboville*. The museum has a wonderful collection of old masters from northern France, as well as a more general collection of 17th and 18th c. French paintings. Among the latter is a lovely portrait by Elisabeth Vigée-Lebrun (1755–1842).

St-Quentin Pop. 65,000

St-Quentin has had an eventful history – 1557, when the town was taken by the Spanish, is perhaps the best known of many important dates. The exceedingly handsome *collegiate church*, dedicated to the town's patron saint, was erected

between the 12th and 15th c.; it was restored and enlarged in the 17th c. and again in the 20th c. The various phases of its architectural history can be appreciated best of all from the bell-tower. Although the 34-m-high nave was not built until the 15th c. the earlier double transepts and the ambulatory with its chapels secure for the church a deserved place among the great cathedrals. Some priceless panes of stained glass dating from the first half of the 13th c. have survived in the choir; the organ case is Baroque.

The finest secular building in the town is the Late Gothic *town hall*. The *Musée Antoine Lécuyer* possesses, in addition to 18th, 19th and 20th c. French paint-

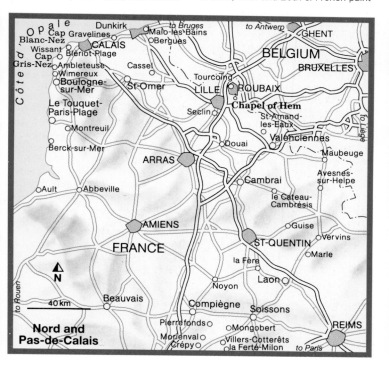

Nord and Pas-de-Calais

ings, an exquisite collection of seventy-eight portraits in pastel by the painter Quentin de la Tour (1704–88), which form a complete 'Who's Who?' of the notables of his day. The portraits are more than merely technically skilled representations – de la Tour's subjects are real people brought vividly to life. The *Musée d'Entomologie* (a museum of insects, with an emphasis on butterflies) is reputed to possess as many as 600,000 specimens, of which more than 100,000 are on display.

 Diamant, 14 Place de la Basilique, tel. 23 64 19 19; *Président*, 6 Rue Dachery, tel. 23 62 69 77.

Cambrai Pop. 37,000

Cambrai lies on the Scheldt – still navigable at this point – and is situated in Hainaut. It is an archbishopric; the cathedral church of *Notre-Dame* is an 18th c. building which has seen several alterations. Of most interest in the church are the grisailles (1760) to be found in the transept chapels. In the apsidal chapel is the tomb of Fénelon (1651–1715), famous theologian and pedagogue, quarrelsome pietist and author of Utopian political works.

In the 17th c. church of *St-Géry* there are some truly diverting Baroque choir screens (now moved to the nave) and a major painting by Rubens, *The Entombment of Christ*. The late 17th c. *Chapelle du Grand Séminaire* (seminary chapel) is a perfect example of Jesuit Baroque. The *Maison Espagnole* (the Spanish house), a half-timbered building with unusual 16th c. carvings, is now the Tourist Office. In the same area are a number of 17th and 18th c. mansions in one of which the *Musée Municipal* is to be found. Besides sculptures there are some very fine Flemish and French paintings there, including contemporary works.

 L'Escargot, 10 Rue Général de Gaulle, tel. 27 81 24 54.

Lewarde. Anyone with an interest in mining, and its history in the Valenciennes area, should make a point of visiting the Mining Centre at Lewarde, where the mine was worked until 1971. The centre has a number of very instructive displays, including an exhibition which tells 'the 345-million-year story of coal', and you can learn all about the life of a miner, or even be taken down the pit.

Valenciennes Pop. 41,000

The chief town of the county of Henegouwen in the Spanish Netherlands, Valenciennes fell into French hands in 1677, thereafter becoming the county town of French Hainaut. Its ramparts have long since given way to wide boulevards encircling a town so steeped in culture that it was once known as the 'Athens of the North'. Jean-Baptiste Pater and, more especially, Antoine Watteau are the town's most celebrated sons, and both are represented by outstanding paintings in the *Musée des Beaux-Arts*. The emphasis of the museum is on Flemish and French painters – Rubens and Bosch are among them – but it also includes works by the sculptor Carpeaux. The 17th c. *Jesuit College* owns an important library. The Jesuit church, now called *St-Nicolas*, has a splendid 18th c. façade. The nave and choir of *St-Géry*, on the other hand, display elements of purest Gothic.

 L'Alberoi, station restaurant, tel. 27 46 86 30.

St-Amand-les-Eaux. There are some superb survivals of Flemish Baroque to be found in this little town, especially

Musée des Beaux-Arts, Valenciennes

what remains of the façade of the *abbey church* with its five orders, one above the other, and 82-m tower. The original abbey dated from the 7th c. but it was beautifully refashioned in the Baroque style in the 17th c. The tower now houses a *pottery museum* to delight the eye (some 500 pieces from St-Amand) and a forty-eight-bell carillon to delight the ear. The former entrance pavilion to the abbey is known as the *Echevinage* (the Aldermen's House) because, besides being the abbot's lodge, it was also where the mayor and aldermen used to meet. It is charming and worth seeing.

Seclin, just to the south of Lille, also has its examples of Flemish Baroque, including the brickwork and rich sculptural ornamentation of its 17th c. *hospital.* Also impressive is the 13th c. collegiate church of *St-Piat.* The tomb of its patron saint – martyred in the 3rd c. – is to be found in the crypt of this pilgrim church. There are interesting capitals in the nave.

Lille Pop. 158,000
Administrative centre of the Nord department

Lille is the capital of French Flanders and main urban centre of northern France. Including the population of the surrounding countryside and the towns of *Roubaix* and *Tourcoing,* with which it is now merged, its inhabitants number about 1.1 million.

Lille's origins can be traced back to the 9th c. when Baldwin, Count of Flanders, built a castle on an island in the River Deûle. First mention of a town here, 'Insula', comes in a document of 1066. Civic status was granted in 1127 and the city quickly gained in importance through its woollen industry before being occupied by French troops for the first time in 1297. With the marriage of Margaret of Flanders to Philip the Bold, Lille passed into the hands of the dukes of Burgundy and a period of increasing prosperity began. Having become a Habsburg possession in 1477 it was captured by Louis XIV in

Summer carnival in Cassel

1667, and was expanded by Vauban into one of the most important fortresses in France. Although the city resisted Louis XIV for nine days, in each of the two World Wars it fell to the Germans after just three.

 Sightseeing in Lille

This lively, cosmopolitan city, with its large university, theatres and opera house, trade fair and autumn festivals, has style, atmosphere and sophistication.

Lille *Old Town* abounds in historic buildings with the stamp of Flemish Baroque, as well as early town mansions like the late 15th c. *Palais Ribour* which today houses the Tourist Office. A little further on, past more old mansions, is the *Grande Place* (now named after General de Gaulle). This is the heart of the city and can boast France's largest bookshop, 'Furet du Nord', and Lille's most beautiful building, the *Vieille Bourse* (the old stock exchange). Further squares follow, each in its way typical: they include the late 19th c. *Place*

du Théâtre, the predominantly 18th c. *Place du Lion d'Or*, and the Baroque *Place Louise-de-Bettignies* with its lovely house at no. 29. There are more delightful and extremely varied houses (some now turned into antique-shops) in the *Rue de la Monnaie*, in which stands also the *Hospice Comtesse*, the most famous of the city's historic hospices. Rebuilt after a fire in 1468 and enlarged over subsequent centuries, this impressive building with its remarkable ward and old chapel has since been converted into a *museum of local history*. Here you can learn all sorts of interesting things about everyday life in 17th and 18th c. Lille.

Although the city's churches are not of major importance some are still worth seeing, particularly the *Eglise St-Maurice*, a hall church begun in the 15th c. but finished only in the 19th c. *Ste-Marie-Madeleine*, begun in 1675, has a central dome, while the austere tower of *Ste-Catherine* dominates the charming Rue Royale.

Vauban's greatest fortress, the *citadel*, is still used by the army. It took 2,000 labourers the three years from 1668 to 1670 to lay its 60 million bricks.

Lille has a great many *museums* devoted to a wide variety of subjects — for example, religious art, Egyptian culture, natural history and geology, industry and commerce. The *Musée des Beaux-Arts* in the Place de la République is one of the largest in France. The picture gallery contains a collection of Late Gothic masters (whom the French call *primitifs*), as well as Flemish and Dutch paintings among which are some excellent works by well-known names. French, Italian and Spanish artists are also well represented, the Impressionists in particular, and there are some exciting contemporary works. Lille's smallest museum, dedicated to its greatest son, is *de Gaulle's birthplace* in the Rue Princesse.

 Lutterbach, 10 Rue Faidherbe, tel. 20 55 13 74; *Le Féguide*, Place Gare, tel. 20 06 15 50; *Le Restaurant*, 1 Place Sébastopol, tel. 20 57 05 05.

Around Lille

Roubaix's one really interesting building – the 1958-built chapel of *Hem* – is 7 km from Lille. The stained-glass work is by Alfred Manessier, one of the best-known contributors to the radical revival of Christian art in France in the 1950s.

Cassel. A detour west of the motorway leads to this seemingly timeless village (pop. 2,000) prettily situated on a hill. A fine Late Gothic *church* – not as yet the responsibility of any department for preserving ancient monuments, apparently – adjoins the spacious Grande Place, as do the beautiful *Hôtel de la Noble Cour* and a *museum* (the former having original furnishings dating from the time of its building in the 16th and 17th c.).

Esquelbecq's Grande Place, Late Gothic *hall church* and unspoilt *château* impart a picture-book Flemish atmosphere to this small village.

Bergues is another picturesque village. It suffered badly in 1940 but has since been painstakingly restored. The *Musée Municipal* has some interesting paintings and drawings and, on the floor above, a collection of birds and insects.

Dunkirk Pop. 74,000

French since 1662 when Charles II of England sold it to Louis XIV, and always something of a pawn in struggles between European powers, Dunkirk was almost 80% destroyed in the Second World War. It has risen like a phoenix from the ashes of war to become France's third largest port. The fact that the Flemish canal network converges on Dunkirk gives the town an importance over and above that of a mere sea port. A boat trip round the harbour, a walk through the town and a 'circum-navigation' by car are all to be recommended. Among the main sights are the *Musée d'Art Contemporain* (set in a garden dotted with modern sculptures, and interesting more for the bold architecture of its exterior and open-plan interior than for its somewhat haphazard collection of modern art) and the *Musée des Beaux-Arts* which has Flemish, Dutch and French paintings as well as a section on Dunkirk in the Second World War. *Malo-les-Bains*, a former bathing resort which has now been incorporated into Dunkirk, unfortunately suffers from a surfeit of concrete buildings.

 Hirondelle, Malo-les-Bains, tel. 28 63 17 65; *Richelieu*, station restaurant, tel. 28 66 52 13; *La Meunerie*, 6 km away in Téteghem, tel. 28 26 01 80.

Laon to Calais

This route follows the one from Laon to Dunkirk as far as Cambrai. Thereafter it is only once you are beyond Arras (or beyond Douai if you keep more to the east) that there are any worthwhile detours to be made.

Douai Pop. 44,000

Originally a Late Roman settlement, Douai acquired civic status in the latter part of the 12th c. Its university (founded in 1562) was transferred to Lille 100 years ago. Douai is famous for the 64-m-high tower on its *town hall* (1400), with its imaginative crowning piece (a gilded bronze lion with banner) and sixty-two-bell carillon. A number of *hôtels* in Louis XV and Louis XVI styles, the *theatre façade* from the same period, and the *Palais de Justice* – once the seat of the Flanders parliament – give the town more of a French than a Flemish flavour, though the *Hôtel d'Abancourt-Montmorency* with its Renaissance façade does indeed bear witness to a Flemish past. This building is part of the former charterhouse, a magnificent 16th to 18th c. ensemble now housing a comprehensive *museum* with a gallery of Flemish and French paintings, sculptures and pottery; adjacent to this is a cloister and an elegant chapter-house.

Arras Pop. 45,000
Administrative centre of the Pas-de-Calais department

Founded originally by the Celts on the right bank of the River Scarpe, Arras became a bishopric in the 5th c. and was fought over time and again before eventually becoming French in the mid-17th c. The town's most famous son is undoubtedly Robespierre. Its historic buildings – for instance the Late Gothic *town hall*, complete with tower, in the Petite Place (the so-called Place des Héros), and the Flemish *gabled houses* in the enormous Grande Place next to it – were badly damaged in the First World War and have all been rebuilt. The town's *Musée des Beaux-Arts* with its variety of interesting exhibits is housed in the former abbey of *St-Vaast* which, in the mid-18th c., was enlarged to form a huge monastery complex. Worth seeing are the refectory and the small and large cloisters, as well as the adjoining cathedral.

 Astoria, 12 Place Foch, tel. 21 71 08 14.

Béthune is another of those little Flemish towns laid out around its Grande Place and its *beffroi* (belfry), here, rather unusually, a solitary, imposing tower some 30 m high.

Lillers. Anyone who admires the Romanesque art so widespread and well preserved in neighbouring Normandy will also find a rare example of it here. The church of *St-Omer*, built in the 12th c. (and, where not original, cleverly restored), has a fine arrangement of arches in the nave.

Aire-sur-la-Lys is a picturesque small town whose prosperity in the 16th and 17th c. under Spanish rule is reflected in its buildings, for example in the richly decorated *Bailliage* (bailiff's house) in the Grande Place. Also worth a visit is the mainly Late Gothic collegiate church of *St-Pierre*, 104 m long and with a beautiful early 16th c. tower resembling the tower of Notre-Dame in St-Omer. Another of the town's churches, *St-Jacques*, has a lively Jesuit Baroque façade.

St-Omer Pop. 16,000
This medieval weaving-town, which from the 7th c. onwards grew up around the abbey of St-Bertin, finally became part of France in 1677. Delightful old streets with fine houses, as well as some unusual sights, make it a place well worth staying in.

The basilica of *Notre-Dame* deserves recognition as one of the most important northern French churches outside Picardy. Built between 1200 (the choir) and the mid-15th c., it is 100 m long, 30 m wide, and 23 m high, the tower on the façade being 50 m tall but no wider than a house. All the variations of Gothic style over the centuries can be seen here. The matchless *furnishings* include ornate screens in the aisle chapels, alabaster reliefs, Gothic sculptures and Baroque paintings.

In the nearby *Hôtel Sandelin* there is a fascinating *museum* with furnished salons, an art gallery, superb Romanesque items and Delft-ware, all displayed in the elegant surroundings of a pre-Revolution town mansion. The interior of the former *Jesuit Chapel*, an outstanding example of early Jesuit Baroque, also warrants a visit. Among St-Omer's other attractions are the Gothic ruins of *St-Bertin*, the *Ancien Bailliage* (old bailiff's house) in the Place Foch, the *Natural History Museum* and, occupying the buildings of a former castle 7 km to the west, the *Abbaye St-Paul-de-Wisques*. From there you drive on through *Ardres* with its curious three-cornered Grande Place and continue to Calais.

Calais Pop. 76,000

Situated at the narrowest point of the English Channel (Dover is only 34 km away), Calais, France's premier passenger port, is famous for the 'Six Burghers of Calais' and Auguste Rodin's statues of them. A few weeks after the Battle of Crécy in 1346 — usually taken to be the start of the Hundred Years War — Edward III crossed from England and laid siege to Calais for eight months, to little avail. Hunger, however, eventually forced the inhabitants of the encircled town to give themselves up. Six burghers made a penitential procession barefoot and in hair shirts, thus preventing a massacre in the town. Calais remained in English hands long after the end of the Hundred Years War. Not until 1558,

The town hall, Calais

after a brief period of Spanish Habsburg rule, did it become part of France. Cruelly devastated in the Second World War, Calais today is a modern town which has as yet developed little character.

Rodin's bronze group *The Burghers of Calais* is one of the world's most famous works of sculpture. It stands in the square in front of the town hall. The *Musée des Beaux-Arts et de la Dentelle* has a collection of old masters and some good modern sculpture, as well as an exhibition tracing the development of the lacemaking industry. The *lighthouse*, built in 1848 (271 steps!), provides a marvellous panorama over the town and harbour, with views of the citadel and the very large church of *Notre-Dame*, the latter built in the English Gothic style of the 13th and 14th c. A concrete bunker constructed by the Germans and still known locally as the 'Blockhaus' contains a small *war museum*. Calais is surrounded by good bathing beaches, especially to the west. Nearby, in *Sangatte*, is the entrance of the new 'Eurotunnel' (see page 9).

George V, 36 Rue Royale, tel. 21 97 68 00; *Le Channel*, 3 Bd de la Résistance, tel. 21 34 42 30.

The Burghers of Calais *by Rodin*

The coasts of Nord and Pas-de-Calais

The great scenic variety of the coast which stretches from Dunkirk to Ault — to the border of Haute Normandie, in other words — is revealed only occasionally to anyone in a car. The road seldom hugs the coast, and even from a few hundred metres away, never mind five or so kilometres, it is the inland landscape which makes its impression on the traveller. During the short holiday season very few of the towns along this coast become overcrowded. So pronounced is the difference between high and low tide that it entirely governs life on the beach. Anyone seeking to avoid that sort of problem should head for one of the large bathing centres with their artificial landscapes of outdoor lakes and indoor pools.

The Opal Coast and its environs

If you drive from Malo-les-Bains and Dunkirk (see page 39) through Gravelines and Calais (see page 41) you come to the *Côte d'Opale*, as the Channel coast of Pas-de-Calais is known thanks to its lovely opal light.

Gravelines's main attractions are its old fortifications and the Late Gothic church of *St-Willibrod*. From here *Blériot-Plage*, a pleasant bathing beach, extends as far as Cap Blanc-Nez.

Cap Blanc-Nez, 134 m high, affords a fine view. Continue to Wissant, which has a sheltered beach, and then to Cap Gris-Nez where the cliffs are even more impressive.

Cap Gris-Nez. The whole area is peppered with concrete defence works erected by the Germans. They have a sleepy air about them now, some of them half sunk into the ground and almost overgrown. One of the blockhouses, large enough to be visible for miles around, has been turned into the *Musée du Mur de l'Atlantique*.

Ambleteuse, with its rock-guarded beach abounding in mussels and shrimps, is mainly attractive for fishing, in both sea and river.

Wimereux is one of the more fashionable little spots on the coast. Here the turn of the century has left its curious architectural signature around and on the beach.

On the way to nearby Boulogne it is quite impossible to miss the *Colonne de la Grande Armée*, a 53-m-high monument started in 1804 in honour of Napoleon. You can climb to the top for a superb all-round view, including right across the Channel to England.

Boulogne-sur-Mer Pop. 49,000

This Channel port at the mouth of the River Liane has been a gateway to the world ever since Roman times. From here the Romans launched their conquest of Britain over 2,000 years ago, while today Boulogne is France's second largest passenger port and the largest fishing port in the whole of Europe.

La ville haute (the upper town), entry to which is through the *Porte des Dunes*, is still a little world of its own, enclosed by medieval ramparts and dominated by its castle. In the *Place de la Résistance* the *library* (in a 17th c. convent building) and the massive 13th c. *belfry* stand out. The 18th c. *town hall* and the *Hôtel Desandrouins* give charm and character to the neighbouring Place Godefroy-de-Bouillon at the crossing point of the upper town's chief roads. The almost too grand 19th c. domed *cathedral* in the Rue de Lille (where there are also several little restaurants)

A café in Boulogne

conceals a whole 'underworld' of passages and chambers. Some parts are Roman, others Romanesque, and there is a well-endowed treasury.

Worth seeing in the lower town if you have plenty of time are the *museum* — with collections of antiquities and 19th c. French paintings — and the church of *St-Nicolas*.

 Plage, 14 Bd Ste-Beuve, tel. 21 31 45 35.

Le Touquet-Paris-Plage. It's a matter of opinion whether this little town is really worth the journey, but many French people clearly think it is. Dating from the late 19th c. and with a present population of 5,500, it is an elegant, well-kept, fashionable and very Parisian bathing resort, but correspondingly expensive and overcrowded in the season. It has a lovely beach, shady woods and facilities for every kind of sport.

Montreuil, though, with its enormous citadel constructed over many centuries and the *Eglise St-Saulve* — Romanesque in its beginnings but Gothic in completion and blessed with an elab-

orately furnished 18th c. interior — is definitely worth the detour. In the *Hôtel-Dieu Chapel*, a Late Gothic annexe to the hospital, the 17th c. interior furnishings of heavy, dark wood have been preserved in their entirety.

Berck-sur-Mer. Strung out along the final stretch of the Côte d'Opale are ten more resorts. Each has its own charm and a lot to offer in the way of water sports and riding. Best endowed of all is Berck-sur-Mer, more informal, less pretentious, and (naturally enough) better value than Le Touquet.

Abbeville, pop. 26,000, has a Late Gothic church, the *Eglise St-Vulfran* which flaunts its greatest treasures on its exterior — three porches decorated with fine though comparatively late figures, and the famous carved Renaissance doors of the central entrance. The *Musée Boucher-de-Perthes* has collections of paintings, silver, ivory and prehistoric finds. Outside the town stands the enchanting and beautifully preserved *Château de Bagatelle* (1752), perfectly embodying an early industrialist's dream of the genteel country holiday.

Fishermen at Etretat

Normandy

The oriental saying that the journey is the destination is particularly true of a holiday in Normandy. Unless you are quite literally making a pilgrimage, Rouen, Caen, Bayeux and even France's most famous shrine Mont-St-Michel are not so much termini as remarkable stages on a rewarding itinerary.

Normandy is accordingly dealt with here in a number of sections. The first, *Le Tréport to Cabourg*, traces the continuation of the Pas-de-Calais coast into Normandy, its scenic highlight being the strange chalk cliffs of Etretat. Next comes *The Seine Valley: Vernon to Rouen and Le Havre*, describing one of the loveliest of French river valleys. The section on *Evreux to Bayeux* is full of Normandy's history, with the world-famous Bayeux tapestry providing a fitting climax. Then comes *East to west across southern Normandy*, a journey through the land of horses, woods and pastures. *The Normandy Bocage* follows the Route du Fromage through Calvados and Suisse Normande, while the austere charm of the Cotentin peninsula with its extensive west coast is the subject of the final section, *The Cotentin peninsula and Mont-St-Michel*.

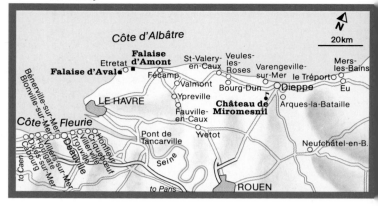

Le Tréport to Cabourg

Le Tréport lies on the boundary between Picardy and Normandy at the mouth of the River Bresle and forms almost a single town with *Mers-les-Bains* on the opposite, east side of the river. Le Tréport's attractions include beautiful beaches, a seafront promenade, a casino, a heated seawater swimming pool, and a superb panorama from the Calvaire des Terrasses (you can drive up to this if you would rather not climb the 378 steps from the town centre).

Eu. Be sure to make the short detour to nearby Eu, sandwiched between woods and the sea. Not only is the exterior of the 12th and 13th c. Gothic church of *Notre-Dame-et-St-Laurent* well worth seeing – it seems to be held together by a web of buttresses and flying buttresses – but the light and spacious interior and the crypt, with some fine ornamentation, also come as a pleasant surprise. Like a number of medieval French churches, Notre-Dame owes its fine state of preservation to the great 19th c. restorer Viollet-le-Duc. The nearby *château*, originally built in the 16th c. but frequently altered since, was one of Louis-Philippe's favourite residences. Beneath its roofscape of chimneys and dormers, the château, still impressive despite all the modifications it has undergone, now houses a museum. The early 17th c. *Chapelle du Collège*, once the chapel of a Jesuit college, boasts the tombs of the Duke and Duchess of Guise.

Dieppe Pop. 35,400

Dieppe, a small but very lively town with houses of many different periods, is seaside resort and port all rolled attractively into one. The handsomely designed and furnished church of *St-Jacques* has been extended a number of times in the centuries since 1250. The *museum* in the 15th c. castle has a collection of paintings and a large maritime section, but is interesting above all for examples of the ivory-work for which Dieppe is famous.

You need to remember, though, that this is the nearest beach resort to Paris and that during the season the roads and cafés are therefore often overcrowded.

Univers, 10 Bd Verdun, tel. 35 84 12 55; *La Mélie*, 2 Grande Rue Pollet, tel. 35 84 21 19.

Around Dieppe. Worth visiting at Arques-la-Bataille not far from Dieppe are the 16th c. *church* and particularly the ruined *castle*. Its keep has crowned the low but craggy hill ever since the 11th c. The late 16th c. *Château de Miromesnil*, 6 km south of Dieppe, has a collection of memorabilia of Guy de Maupassant, one of France's great 19th c. writers, who was born there. Take a good look round the exterior of the château. It has lovely façades, an entrance court, delightful gardens and avenues of trees, and a chapel originally belonging to an earlier building which once stood on the site.

Varengeville-sur-Mer's exceptionally beautiful location has attracted many artists over the years, not all of them painters. The most famous of them, Georges Braque, lies buried in the shadow of the *church*, and one of its windows and the windows in the chapel of *St-Dominique* are his work. The *Manoir d'Ango* is a Renaissance country house in the Italian style, with a splendid *dovecot* in the inner courtyard.

Along the coast between Varengeville and Fécamp — Fécamp being the next largish town you come to — are several small and unsophisticated villages-cum-seaside resorts with a few hundred inhabitants. Some of the village churches are worth a look. The tower of *Bourg-Dun* will certainly catch your eye,

Secular and sacred — architecture of Dieppe

likewise the square tower on the church at *Veules-les-Roses*. There are some delightful coastal views from the cliffs at St-Valery-en-Caux, and a number of war memorials in the vicinity. Such memorials, sadly, are never far away in Normandy.

Fécamp Pop. 21,700

According to tradition Fécamp was blessed in the 7th c. with a relic of Christ's blood, and with its Benedictine monastery and Norman ducal palace the town was once the most important centre of pilgrimage in Normandy. The church of *La Trinité* as it is seen today (its predecessor was destroyed by fire) was built and enlarged in the 12th and 13th c. respectively. Only the later façade detracts in any way from the otherwise complete unity of style exhibited by this massive edifice, built on a scale equalling that of the huge cathedrals of the Île-de-France. With its great length (127 m), and with a crossing-tower which soars to a height of 65 m, its dimensions can really only be compared with those of Notre-Dame in Paris. In the interior the Romanesque and Gothic stylistic elements can be clearly distinguished, but the enlargement was nevertheless subtly handled. The interior furnishings completed in the 18th c. are in keeping with the setting.

The curious ruins of the former palace of the dukes of Normandy, opposite La Trinité, are not open to the public. The *Musée Municipal* has a most varied collection of paintings, ceramics, etc. displayed on four floors, while the *Musée Bénédictine*, housed in a building at once overwhelming and grotesque (the creation of a 19th c. *nouveau riche*), brings together a first-class art collection and 19th c. exhibits related to the marketing of the famous liqueur.

 Angleterre, 93 Rue Plage, tel. 35 28 01 60.

Valmont. A detour is necessary if you are to visit this pretty little town with its *castle* and the remains of a 12th c. Benedictine abbey. The abbey was destroyed by fire in the Gothic period but rebuilt. The *Lady Chapel* with its beautiful windows was built during the Renaissance and the convent buildings date from the 17th c.

Yvetot's church of *St-Pierre,* with its monumental wall of stained glass designed in 1956 by Max Ingrand, bears witness to the extraordinary, sudden reappearance of religious architecture in 1950s France. Important examples of this revival can be found all over the country.

Ypreville. Anyone who happens by this little village will find a mighty fortified tower on its church. In all other respects the church appears in the guise of a typical turn-of-the-century renovation, though with one or two old pieces of statuary and some very moving stained glass windows.

Inland the countryside here is idyllic and quite unspoilt. The farms lie hidden behind their sheltering 'palisades', the straight avenues of trees which are the last remaining vestiges of the natural fortifications abounding in Norman times. Cattle doze in the hollows and on the hillsides, and at every corner a blaze of sweet-smelling roses is revealed. Just being here in this lovely part of the country is peaceful and relaxing.

The country-style restaurants and especially the rather infrequent inns and small hotels are always friendly and, if you happen to strike lucky, can offer extremely good value – the

Auberge de la Durdent in Héricourt-en-Caux for example, tel. 39 96 42 44, and *Du Commerce* in Fauville-en-Caux, tel. 35 96 71 22.

The chalk cliffs of Etretat

After Mont-St-Michel the chalk cliffs at Etretat are Normandy's most famous landmark – certainly they must be the region's most widely recognised natural feature. The *Falaise d'Aval* immediately west of Etretat (perhaps the most famous cliff formation of them all) and the *Falaise d'Amont* to the east are unique with their bizarrely shaped arches and pinnacles. Layers of chalk and flint reacting differently to the seawater have produced distinctive bands in the cliffs which the ever-changing light renders still more fascinating. But the days have long since gone when Monet, Boudin and many other artists, as well as the very first tourists, studied

and painted these wonders of nature in an atmosphere of tranquillity and near reverence. Etretat today is vastly overcrowded, as is the town beach (which has also suffered from overbuilding). Things improve, however, when you take the footpath along the cliffs. In Etretat itself, pop. 1,600, the church of *Notre-Dame* provides a good example of Romanesque building, with geometric capitals in the first six bays of the nave (completed, however, in the Gothic style). Elsewhere in the town the timber-built *covered market*, nicely restored, has great character.

 Angleterre, Av George V, tel. 35 27 01 65.

The so-called *Côte d'Albâtre*, the alabaster coast, ends at Etretat. Continue via Le Havre to the further side of the Seine estuary and Honfleur.

The famous Falaise d'Aval chalk cliffs at Etretat

Honfleur

Honfleur Pop. 8,400

In the 16th c. Canada became a colony settled mainly by seamen from Honfleur. In the 19th c. Honfleur itself became a colony, this time of artists, primarily painters. Today the little town is a colony for tourists from all over the world. What there is to see is still charming enough, however: the inner harbour encircled by tall, mostly dark-coloured, narrow-fronted houses with, at its entrance, *La Lieutenance*

(16th c.), the former residency of the governor of Honfleur; the old streets climbing up the hill; and, joining the harbour and the Old Town, the *Place Ste-Catherine* with its famous *sailors' church* of the same name. Inside the church the timber vaulting consists of two almost identical wooden 'hulls' placed keel-uppermost over the twin naves. The whole structure, in fact, is of timber. Across the square the detached belfry, also made of wood, houses a number of religious items.

Three museums bring Old Honfleur to life in their different ways: the *Musée Eugène Boudin* is devoted primarily to paintings by Boudin himself and others of the Honfleur School; the *Musée de la Marine* in the former church of St-Etienne has a collection of everything to do with the port and seafaring; finally, housed in what used to be the prison, the *Musée d'Art Populaire* contains reconstructions of Norman work-places and dwellings, as well as costumes, etc.

 Au P'tit Mareyeur, 4 Rue Haute, tel. 31 98 84 23.

The Côte de Grâce

Taking its name from the chapel of *Notre-Dame-de-la-Grâce*, this enchanting stretch of coast immediately to the west of Honfleur affords marvellous vistas. From high above both sea and Seine you can look across to Le Havre and up river to the Tancarville Bridge. The 17th c. chapel takes its name in turn from the reputedly miraculous statue of 'Notre-Dame-de-la-Grâce', before which seafarers bound for Canada used to leave tiny ex-voto model ships. Along the coast at *Criqueboeuf* there is a Romanesque church, and in the pretty seaside resort of *Villerville* a church tower from the same period. After that the road, bordered by lush greenery, drops down to the fine sandy beach at Trouville.

The Côte Fleurie
Trouville Pop. 6,000

This elegant bathing resort marks the beginning of the *Côte Fleurie*, which extends westwards as far as Cabourg. The name is fitting tribute to this, the loveliest and undoubtedly most popular part of the Normandy coast. Trouville is rather more down-to-earth than its twin, the adjoining town of Deauville, being not quite so ultra-fashionable and expensive; it is also not quite as lifeless out of season as other resorts. It has an *aquarium* on the beach with salt- and freshwater fish, and the *Musée Montebello* has exhibits tracing the history of the resort and its art.

 Carmen, 24 Rue Carbot, tel. 31 88 35 43.

The seaside resort of Trouville

Place de Morny, Deauville

Deauville Pop. 4,800

You should have no illusions about these comparatively large and famous seaside resorts, particularly Deauville. To really enjoy yourself here you need a large purse, and a taste for an old-fashioned kind of luxury holiday. Those who still indulge themselves with this sort of holiday in Deauville want above all to mix with their own kind, whether it be at the casino or in the Second Empire splendour of the rambling old hotels (modernised, of course, to the highest of standards).

Lunch-time rendezvous

A walk through the town – at its liveliest from July to September – reveals an odd mix of architectural styles of the late 19th c., when anyone with money aspired to his own distinctive seaside villa in the vicinity of the beach. The beach itself, however, remains firmly in the hands of the hotels. Deauville basks in its own limelight, with its horse-racing, American film festival, golf tournaments, congresses and every kind of gala event. With this sort of resort you have to make a choice: you either take a quick look round in passing, or you stay and accept the financial consequences!

✗🍴 *Normandy* with *La Potinière* restaurant, tel. 31 88 09 21.

Bénerville to Houlgate. The little resorts of *Bénerville-sur-Mer* and *Blonville-sur-Mer* have lovely beaches of fine sand. *Villers-sur-Mer* is a bathing resort with a casino; its 5-km-long beach extends as far as the cliffs known as the *Vaches Noires*. Beyond them lies *Houlgate*, a particularly popular beach resort with attractive countryside behind.

Dives-sur-Mer, facing Cabourg across the Dives estuary, lays claim to a special place in history, for it was from here that William the Bastard set out to conquer England. The 15th and 16th c. *covered market* is a *tour de force* of oak beams, while the late medieval church of *Notre-Dame de Dives* is notable for its striking combination of lightness and massive strength. The *Village Guillaume le Conquérant*, a fine 16th c. inn, has been turned into craft shops.

Cabourg is laid out in the shape of a half moon, its streets fanning outwards like a peacock's tail. This is Marcel Proust's town, to which the great French novelist came, from childhood onwards, in search of relief from his asthma. Devotees of Proust can wander through the 'Pullman Grand Hôtel', its halls and rooms – including the 'huge and wonderful aquarium', as Proust called the restaurant – already familiar to them from *Remembrance of Things Past*.

Avenue de la Mer, Cabourg

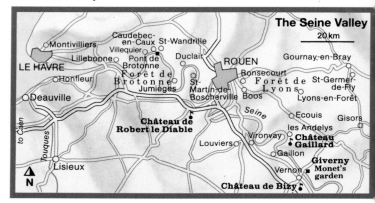

The Seine Valley: Vernon to Rouen and Le Havre

The Seine Valley

Before opening out funnel-shaped to the sea at Le Havre the valley of the Seine forms one of the loveliest river landscapes in France. The impressive and at the same time graceful river cuts more or less diagonally across Haute Normandie.

Almost 200 years ago Napoleon described Paris, Rouen and Le Havre as forming one city, with the Seine its single thoroughfare. This seems even more true today. Haute Normandie is immensely important economically, a

Traditional farmhouse

status to which Rouen and Le Havre, two of France's primary ports, make no small contribution.

However, for anyone travelling the Normandy section of the Seine, journey's end should be Honfleur (page 50), on the west side of the estuary, still picturesque and unspoilt despite the tourists. The road to the estuary sometimes follows the river's meandering course, sometimes veers away to shortcut one of its often pronounced and narrow-necked loops. It runs through pleasant, varied scenery, a landscape of hills, castles, magnificent abbeys, and charming little towns with old-fashioned hotels and chugging ferries, small museums and lively market-places. It passes through Rouen and, as it nears the estuary, through the Brotonne Forest and nature reserve. Long days spent here in the Seine Valley, enjoying every combination of art and nature that anyone could possibly desire, make for a holiday that does the soul good – and the further north from Paris you go the cheaper it becomes. With great ocean-going ships gliding by, with romantic medieval castles, and with some distinctly good food even by Normandy standards, the heart of Normandy has surely never disappointed anyone.

The Seine

The Seine, 776 km long and third longest river in France after the Loire and the Rhône, seemed tortuous even to the Celts. They called it *Squan*, which the Romans turned into *Sequana*. From its source – on the Plateau de Langres in Burgundy – to where it debouches into the sea, the Seine drops only 471 m. Just up river from Vernon on the Normandy border its bed is no more than 16 m above sea level, and even before it reaches Paris the slow-flowing river has already begun to carve its massive bends. Despite this shallow gradient the river has still cut downwards for 100 m, deep into the chalky substrate. From Vernon to Le Havre is only 90 km as the crow flies, but the river winds for more than twice that distance before arriving at the sea – 210 km of meandering through its 12- to 14-km-wide valley. Stronger currents on the outsides of the huge bends make the so-called concave banks the most suitable for harbour development and cultivation, by preventing the deposition of shingle. The alluvial sands and shingle of the convex bends in contrast support extensive areas of forest. In earlier times the Brotonne Forest was used as a hunting ground by the Frankish kings. Today it is part of the Brotonne Regional Park (*Parc naturel régional de Brotonne*), jointly established in 1974 by forty-seven local districts (see page 66).

The Seine bore

Until the middle of the last century the Seine bore *(le mascaret)*, a tidal phenomenon, was a source of fear, adventure, and popular diversion. Many a curious onlooker was attracted by this spectacle of nature, a regular occurrence around the equinoxes. So great was the mass of tidal water from the estuary forcing its way up river on the flood that the Seine's own current was reversed. A gigantic wave higher than a house used to form where the natural flow of the river came up against the water racing in from the sea. Between 1830 and 1852 more than 100 ships are reputed to have been overwhelmed, not to mention the people who fell victim to it. Among the ships lost in earlier days was the *Télémach* which sank in 1790 near Quillebeuf; it was said to be carrying the French crown jewels to England for safe-keeping during the Revolution.

Since 1846 the Seine has been regulated, so nowadays the bore is much smaller, appearing only at spring tides.

Claude Monet's lily pond

Vernon to Rouen and Le Havre

Vernon Pop. 23,000

Founded by the Norsemen in the 9th c., Vernon is prettily positioned between its forest (of the same name) and the Seine, here dotted with delightful wooded islands. The church of *Notre-Dame*, in origin a Late Romanesque building but altered a number of times up to the 16th c., makes a distinctive feature on the town's skyline. The façade is Late Gothic, as also is the nave which, unusually, is higher than the transepts and chancel.

The varied collections of the *Musée A.-G. Poulain* include paintings by the great Impressionist Claude Monet who lived not far away, in Giverny.

In Giverny itself you will find the artist's house, his studio, and, most important of all, his famous *gardens* which, linked by an underpass, extend both sides of the road. This is a place of pilgrimage for all Monet fans, where the memorabilia are actually growing and need to be watered and pruned. (See also page 20.)

The Château de Bizy, away from the Seine at the western side of Vernon, stands in a superb park. Several magnificent rooms in the elegant 18th c. building are open to the public.

Gaillon (pop. 5,800), 14 km north-west of Vernon, is a typical little Normandy town. It has some *half-timbered houses* and a *castle* which for a long time was in the possession of the archbishops of Rouen. The castle gatehouse, flanked by towers, is pure Renaissance in style. Beyond Gaillon, *en route* for Rouen, the ancient cloth-making town of Louviers on the left bank of the Seine should be the next port of call.

Louviers Pop. 19,400

The town is delightfully placed between the valleys of three rivers, the Seine, the Eure and the Iton. Old half-timbered houses add to the character of the area around the church of *Notre-Dame*, which was built between the 13th and 15th c. The south side of the church, in particular, displays some fine examples of Flamboyant architecture; 'lacework in stone' is how the elegant and elaborate carving has been described. With its tombs, priceless Late Gothic figures, old altars and Renaissance windows, the *interior* of the five-naved church also repays unhurried inspection. The history of the town and its cloth-weaving industry is imaginatively presented in the *Musée Municipal*, which also possesses a good ceramics section.

Vironvay, a few kilometres east of Louviers, provides a first view of Château Gaillard, visible from the village church which stands on a hill.

This marks the beginning of a delightful detour on the way to Rouen. The roughly rectangular route takes you some 50 km east of the Seine and back again, first stop being Les Andelys.

Les Andelys Pop. 8,200

At the outermost point of a sharp bend on the Seine, and at a spot as beautiful as it was once strategically favourable, Petit and Grand Andelys have today merged to form the present town. It is a popular watering place (an old-fashioned term which comes to mind over and over again here in the valley of the Seine). The river works its refreshing magic and the little town, well kept and full of charm, has more than its share of interest. With shady footpaths on every side and towered over by one of France's most famous castles, Les Andelys is a rewarding stopping place on any journey along the Seine. The impressive church of *Notre-Dame* was constructed between the 13th and 17th c. The nave dates from the early days of its building while other parts are in the Flamboyant and Renaissance styles. The *Eglise St-Sauveur* was begun even earlier, in the late 12th c. But it is to *Château Gaillard* that Les Andelys primarily owes its character. This mighty castle was raised by Richard the Lionheart in 1196 as a counterbalance to nearby Gisors, the intention being to loosen the French king's hold here in the north. Encircled by two walls and moats, the central keep stands in a dazzlingly beautiful location on a chalk spur, chosen originally of course for its strategic importance. Of the five original defence towers only one is still standing. Tradition has it that the castle was completed within a year, but for all its elaborate defences it had been taken less than a decade later. Try to make sure you visit it in good weather; there is a quite breathtaking view over the Seine.

 Normandie, tel. 32 54 10 52; *Paris,* tel. 32 54 00 33.

Château Gaillard, Les Andelys

Ecouis Pop. 750

8 km north of Les Andelys is the little village of Ecouis, visible from afar amidst the gold and green fields of corn and sugar-beet which chequer the chalk plateau known as the *Vexin*. The somewhat ordinary, though light for its size, post-1300 *collegiate church* possesses at least a dozen outstanding statues dating from the 14th to 17th c. Ten of these date from the time the church was built, when it was decorated with no fewer than fifty-two figures. The almost life-sized figure of Christ Crucified is the only one carved in wood, the rest being sculpted in limestone. None is less than fine, while amongst the very finest are those of St Anne the mother of Mary, St Cecilia, St Mary Magdalene, and the Madonna and Child.

Gisors Pop. 8,900

This, the main town of the Vexin, is dominated by Normandy's most celebrated *castle* after Château Gaillard. Dating from the 12th c. it impresses more by its bulk and extent – the site is laid out as public gardens – than by any sense of history or romance. In contrast, the church of *St-Gervais-et-St-Protais* is unusual, full of originality and with a wealth of interesting detail. Although the chancel was consecrated in 1249, the transepts and nave were still being completed in the 16th c. The result is an unusually successful marriage of Gothic and Renaissance elements. A Renaissance tower staircase leading up to a gallery, columns decorated with remarkable carvings, fascinating 16th c. windows, and sculptures from the second period of building all help to make the interior of the church as interesting as the exterior with its towers and richly ornamented doorways.

St-Germer-de-Fly, north of Gisors on a side-road which turns off a little way before Gournay, has an extremely fine Early Gothic *abbey* with a beautiful chancel and Romanesque altar.

In Gournay-en-Bray visit the church of *St-Hildevert*. Its Romanesque capitals are carved with animal and plant motifs and there are some very early statues in the aisles; the painted wooden figures of the Madonna and the church's patron saint are of particular interest.

Gerberoy. To get to know this pretty, once fortified village you must branch off north-eastwards for some 13 km. In the 19th c. it was 'discovered' by artists who left it even more decorative than before. The church of *St-Pierre* dates from the 15th c.

The Lyons Forest. Heading back towards the Seine you pass through the *Forêt de Lyons*, an area famous for its beech woods, covering almost 11,000 hectares. There are many magnificent old trees of which the best known, the *hêtre de la Bunodière* (the Bunodière beech) is more than 40 m high and has a girth of almost 3.5 m. A large forested area such as this – though the same applies to smaller tracts of other Normandy landscapes – is best explored from a central base where you can find a ready supply of brochures and route maps for even the more modest of the region's sights. The best place to stay here is Lyons-en-Forêt.

Lyons-en-Forêt is a small place with a population of only 730, and still retains its original circular layout. The church of *St-Denis*, part 12th and part 15th c., perfectly reflects the resources of the area, being constructed from wood alternating with flint (see page 8). In the centre of the village, the open-sided 18th c. *covered market* with its splendid timber rafters blends picturesquely with the houses in the square.

Boos is definitely not to be missed by anyone interested in Normandy's dovecots (see page 18). The *colombier* here, built in 1530 from stone, brick and ceramic tiles, is the most unusual of all the buildings bequeathed to posterity by the abbesses of St-Amand-de-Rouen, to whom the land belonged.

At Bonsecours, just outside Rouen, it is worth driving up to the neo-Gothic basilica, a popular place of pilgrimage, to enjoy the magnificent view. From every angle partial views and whole panoramas of the city and the Seine Valley are opened up before you.

Rouen Pop. 105,000
Administrative centre of the Seine-Maritime department

Rouen, the most beautiful city in Normandy – and one of the loveliest in the whole of France – was rebuilt after the terrible destruction of the last war. Large parts of the old and, as it seemed at the time, irreplaceable Rouen, the areas lying between the cathedral and the Seine, were particularly badly hit. The rebuilding, though, has been a success, the wounds have healed, and the 'City of a Hundred Towers' once again displays its wealth of churches and palaces, old streets and squares, half-timbered houses, and museums.

The original founders of old Rouen chose to settle not inside the sheltering loop offered by the Seine, but out in the open, as it were, on the river's right bank. Today, however, the city – like Paris – is divided into a *Rive Gauche* and a *Rive Droite*, six bridges linking the two. From a tourist point of view interest centres almost entirely on the Rive Droite. Rouen, it has to be remembered, is a major industrial city, and there is no escaping the fact. But ports with their

evocative waterfront architecture somehow seem able to get away with it, even when, as here, the dockland area is hardly picturesque. Rouen is the fifth largest French maritime port and third largest river port, capable of handling vessels of up to 140,000 tonnes and container ships of up to 2,000 units.

The population figure given is rather misleading. Greater Rouen consists of twenty-two districts in which about half a million people live. Tourists also come in their numbers, for in this conurbation the Middle Ages and the next millennium are to be found in truly unusual combination. So there is every reason to set aside more than just a few hours for visiting the city. The ideal arrangement in fact is to stay for a few days somewhere in the Seine countryside nearby, making excursions into Rouen by car. It is best to leave your car on the edge of the Old Town – where parking is quite easy – and, depending on your mood or the weather, take a look at Rouen's buildings or its museums. It is not only the pedestrian precincts which make a car superfluous; the Old Town as a whole is best explored on foot. You

The church of Ste-Jeanne-d'Arc in Rouen, built in 1979

can then stroll round at leisure, stopping as you will, constantly finding new things to look at and delighting in the half-timbered houses and the mansions.

History

Under the Celts and Romans Rouen, variously named Ratumacus, Rotomagus and Rotumagos, was already an important trading centre at the crossroads of routes leading to the coast. Saints Niçaise, Mellonius, Romain (who is said to have slain the dragon Gargouille) and Ouen all preached Christianity here in its early days. In 841 and 876 Rouen suffered terribly at the hands of Viking raiders but in 912 the Norseman Rollo was granted the land around Rouen, taking on the obligations of a vassal. He accepted Christianity and was baptised Robert. The old settlement became the centre of his dukedom, and by deepening the Seine here Rollo turned the city into the most important after Paris in the west Frankish empire, an eminence it retained until the 18th c. In 1150 tax and legal privileges were conferred on it and in 1160 Henry II granted it extensive civic rights. In 1315 it became the seat of the diet or council called the Echiquier; later it was that of the regional parliament.

Occupied by Philippe Auguste in 1204 and attaining great economic wealth in the 13th and 14th c., Rouen defended itself vigorously against the English, referred to at the time as the 'Goddons' on account of their use of the oath 'God damn...'. The city eventually fell in 1419, however, during the Hundred Years War, and English rule was established as it was in the whole of northern France. In 1430 the Burgundians were paid by the English to hand over Joan of Arc who had been taken prisoner in the Forest of Compiègne. The year before she had had Charles VII crowned king of France at Reims, and in doing so had given fresh impetus to the French cause. She was accused of heresy by an ecclesiastical court in Rouen and in 1431 the English finally decided that she should burn at the stake. It was another nineteen years before Charles VII was able to recover Rouen, and it was there in 1456 that the judgement against Joan was rescinded.

Half-timbered buildings in Rouen

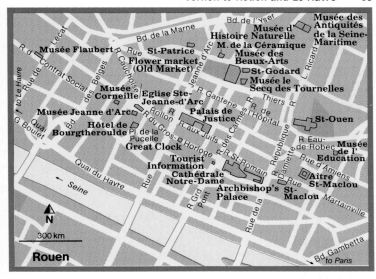

Rouen

She was canonised in 1920 and has since then been patron saint of France.

During the Renaissance Rouen flourished anew under Georges d'Amboise, one of Louis XII's ministers and a papal legate. He was succeeded by a nephew of the same name and then by cardinals of the Bourbon family. The city already had access to the sea through Dieppe, and from 1517 it could also use the newly founded port of Le Havre. Its merchants, famous for their cloth and silks, were soon to be found the world over. In the 18th c. the manufacture and dyeing of cotton also made its appearance, providing keen competition for the Dutch who until then had been undisputed leaders in this craft. With the increasing industrialisation of the 19th c. Rouen gained further in importance through its position on the Seine between Paris and Le Havre.

The city's famous sons include the writers Pierre Corneille and Gustave Flaubert, as well as the painter Théodore Géricault.

A walk round the city

Everywhere in old Rouen you come across half-timbered houses. They were built in great variety ranging from modest town houses to palatial mansions. More than 700 have already been restored, most being located in the 3 km of streets which make up the pedestrian precinct. Half-timbering was used for building in Rouen until the late 18th c., almost always with oak beams. The most lavish and spectacularly ornamented timberwork dates from the 16th c., the time of the Renaissance.

The walk which follows – lasting about three hours – takes you round the most important sights in the Old Town. Start at the *Place de la Cathédrale*, where you will find the Tourist Office opposite the cathedral in a lovely *Renaissance mansion* built in 1510. The cathedral of *Notre-Dame* is considered one of the foremost Gothic churches in France. Begun in the 12th c., actually constructed (after a fire) in the 13th c., completed and furnished in the 15th and 16th c., it conveys, both inside and out, an impression of harmony and grandness of scale, as well as being somewhat unusual.

The towers of the façade are each typical of their period, the *Tour St-Romain*, recently restored to its original height of 82 m, being Early Gothic while the 77-m-high *Butter Tower* is decorated with all the virtuosity of the Flamboyant style. The Butter Tower takes its name from the arrangement which paid for it, by which dispensation was granted allowing the consumption of butter during Lent in return for contributions towards the building (butter being considered a basic necessity by the Normans). The tower has only an octagonal crown in place of a tall spire, so perhaps there were a few skinflints indulging in butter for Lent without making any donation! The *St-Jean* and *St-Etienne* doorways are 12th c., their lovely tympana date from the 13th c., and the central doorway is 16th c.

The *crossing-tower* is 151 m high and thanks to the iron spire cast in 1876 is the tallest church tower in France. It was erected in the 13th c. and raised further in the 16th c. Also notable on the exterior are the doorways to the transepts, the *Portail de la Calende* (13th to 14th c.) on the south side and the *Portail des Libraires* on the north. The latter, reached through the *Cour des Libraires*, was built at the same time but has richer and more exuberant decoration. This includes an incomplete relief on the tympanum depicting the Last Judgement. Both court and doorway owe their names to the booksellers who once had their stalls here.

The *interior* of the cathedral, though clearly dating from a variety of periods, nevertheless appears entirely harmonious. Of greatest beauty is the 13th c.

chancel with its ambulatory, its three chapels, its five brilliantly coloured 13th c. stained-glass windows, and its 11th c. crypt beneath. The central *Chapelle de la Vierge* (Lady Chapel) contains the magnificent Renaissance tombs of Louis de Brézé and the Cardinals d'Amboise.

Just to the north of Notre-Dame is the *Rue St-Romain*, one of the most typical and attractive streets in the Old Town. Its half-timbered houses, some of which are now antique-shops, date from many different centuries. Continuing eastwards, past the *Archbishop's Palace* with its imposing façade, you come to the church of *St-Maclou* built between 1437 and 1517 in the purest Flamboyant Gothic style. There is a marvellous harmony to its five-arched façade, and its Renaissance oak doors are intriguingly carved with a variety of motifs. In the interior are fine examples of 15th and 18th c. craftsmanship.

The *Aître St-Maclou*, located to the east of the chancel, is a medieval plague cemetery. The half-timbered, galleried houses round the inner courtyard are decorated with motifs of the Dance of Death. The buildings are now occupied by the School of Art.

Next retrace your steps to the front of St-Maclou and turn right into *Rue Damiette* which is lined with more half-timbered houses. Continue to the *Place du Lieutenant-Aubert* from where, in the *Rue d'Amiens*, you can see the 16th c. *Hôtel d'Etancourt*, the façade of which is decorated with figures. Carry on further to the *Rue Eau-de-Robec*, the former dyers' yard, where some of the lofts in which the cloth was dried can still be seen, and then beyond to the third of Rouen's important Gothic churches, the collegiate church of *St-Ouen*. Formerly part of a Benedictine abbey, this flawless example of Gothic architecture was begun in 1318 and completed in the 15th c., after the familiar interruption caused by the Hundred Years War. The east end of the church is particularly lovely: the crossing-tower and the chancel with its chapels and buttresses. The interior exudes Gothic inspiration, not just because of its proportions but also by virtue of the light filtering through its stained-glass windows.

Rouen's most important secular building – reached via the Rue de l'Hôpital, the Rue Ganterie and the flower market – is the *Palais de Justice*, started in the late 15th c. on the remains of the synagogue and originally intended for the Exchequer. Following Philip the Fair's expulsion of the Jews from France in 1308 a spice market was established in the old Jewish quarter, and a superb hall was planned to give visual expression to the prosperity of the tradespeople. The façade, increasingly ornate towards the top, manages to preserve a certain lightness and clarity in spite of its profusion of detail. The writer and lawyer Pierre Corneille worked here in the old lawcourts.

The *Rue aux Juifs* and the *Rue Rollon* lead to the *Old Market*, where in 1431 Joan of Arc was burned as a heretic, after a political show trial dressed up as a religious one. The old square is dominated by the modern (1979) church of *Ste-Jeanne-d'Arc*, a spacious, light building with a bold roof construction. The interior has remarkable Renaissance *stained-glass windows* which, having earlier been placed in store, escaped the destruction of Rouen's church of St-Vincent in 1944.

Only a few steps away from here are the *Place de la Pucelle* and the *Hôtel de Bourgtheroulde*, a Late Gothic mansion

with an unpronounceable name (sounding rather like 'Boortrood'), one of a number of buildings which testify to the city's wealth at the beginning of the modern period. Now return in the direction of the cathedral, via the *Rue du Gros-Horloge* where medieval Rouen in the form of more half-timbered houses clusters around the *Great Clock*, probably the city's best-known landmark. In its elaborate Renaissance surround, it is set above an archway spanning the street. The *belfry* next to it, the former clock-tower, retains the original late 14th c. mechanism, together with parts of other clocks, in a small museum. The laborious climb to the top of the tower

St-Maclou, Rouen

The Great Clock, Rouen

brings its reward in the shape of a fine view.

Anyone especially interested in stained-glass windows and prepared to walk further will discover some fine early 16th c. examples in *St-Godard*, while *St-Patrice* has later 16th c. paintings on glass – really a more accurate description of Renaissance windows such as these. Both churches can be found in the immediate vicinity of Rouen's most important museums. The *Musée des Beaux-Arts* has a general collection including some interesting Italian and French paintings, particularly pictures by Géricault who was born in Rouen. The *Musée de la Céramique* traces the development of the city's famous pottery (see page 20). The *Musée le Secq des Tournelles* (the iron-work museum) displays its treasures in a Late Gothic church: 6,000 exhibits dating from Roman times to the 19th c. Wrought-iron grilles and banisters are shown to advantage in the nave and transepts of the former church.

What was once a convent is now the home of the *Musée des Antiquités de la Seine-Maritime*. The collection includes prehistoric finds as well as applied art and items of craftsmanship, among them valuable examples of Romanesque enamelwork and carved Gothic ivories. The *Musée Jeanne d'Arc*, complete with waxworks, and the *Musée Corneille* together pay Rouen's local homage to these national figures. Medicine and natural history are celebrated in the *Musée Flaubert et d'Histoire de la Médecine* and the *Musée d'Histoire Naturelle* respectively, the former dedicated to Gustave Flaubert's father who was a surgeon. The *Musée de l'Education*, in an exceedingly beautiful 15th c. house near the dyers' yard, concentrates on the history of child-rearing and education.

✕️ *Ibis Rouen Centre*, 56 Quai G. Boulet, tel. 35 70 48 18; *Dieppe et rest. Les Quatre Saisons*, Place B. Tissot, tel. 35 71 96 00; *Le Réverbère*, 5 Place de la République, tel. 35 07 03 14; *Le Havre*, 27 Rue Verte, tel. 35 71 46 43.

Ex There are two literary pilgrimages to make from Rouen: to *Corneille's manor house* 8 km to the south-east in *Petit-Couronne*, and to the *Pavillon Flaubert* in *Croisset*. There is now a museum in the one remaining part of the property in which Gustave Flaubert wrote *Madame Bovary*, the novel which caused such a sensation.

Especially in the light of evening, the panoramic views over the 'City of a

Hundred Towers' from the vantage points on the *Corniche* of the *Côte Ste-Catherine* fully repay the drive there.

Château de Robert-le-Diable. Not even noise from the motorway can spoil the lovely view down to the Seine from the ruins of this castle built by the early dukes of Normandy and destroyed in about 1200. The defiant remains are rather more interesting than the scenes of Norman history recreated with wax figures inside the castle. Outside there is an informative reconstruction of a Viking ship.

St-Martin-de-Boscherville Pop. 1,400

This little town can boast one of the finest Romanesque churches in Normandy, the former abbey church of *St-Georges*. Built between 1080 and 1125, it has a surprising purity and unity of style even though the nave and transepts were not vaulted over till the Gothic period. The unadorned façade, the massive central tower with its double arcades and window openings, and the two-storeyed apse make St-Georges a perfect example of High Romanesque Norman architecture. In addition to the church (not always open) there is a Romanesque *chapter-house*, and some remains of even older buildings dating back to Roman times.

Duclair, pop. 3,500, is a pleasant little town where you can cross the Seine by ferry free of charge. The church of *St-Denis* with a Romanesque tower and Gothic chapels has some fine old furnishings and Renaissance windows. The weekly market is one of the liveliest in the area.

Jumièges

The next stop on the so-called *Route des Abbayes* is extremely impressive even though just a ruin. Jumièges abbey, with its main church of *Notre-Dame*, was founded by St Philibert in the 7th c., consecrated on the day after the conquest of England in 1066, and finally abandoned by its last monks during the French Revolution. Afterwards it came to be used as a sort of stone-quarry – the central tower being demolished – until in the mid-19th c. it was saved in its present form. Today it is one of the most delightful places in Normandy.

The spires have long since gone but the square towers, rising still to a height of 43 m and, with their octagonal tops, seeming to rotate skywards, are eye-catching features on an unforgettable façade, behind which the lofty roofless space is open to light and air. The remains of the transept, one side of the lantern tower, the Gothic choir, the striking ruins of the neighbouring Carolingian-Gothic church of *St-Pierre* and the chapter-house together form a close-knit and still recognisable ensemble of monumental medieval buildings. The 17th c. abbot's lodge (*logis abbatial*) maintains a respectful distance. In the parish church of *St-Valentin* in the village of Jumièges the choir and ambulatory are particularly worth seeing.

St-Wandrille

Also worth a visit are the ruins of the abbey church of Fontenelle – later called the *Abbaye-St-Wandrille* after its founder – on a site still occupied by Benedictine monks. Open to the public are the 14th c. church ruins, the Late Gothic cloister and the present church, a former 13th c. tithe barn brought in pieces from Neuville-du-Bosc by the monks and reassembled. On the edge of the abbey park is the chapel of *St-Saturnin*, a small 10th c. shrine with a cloverleaf-shaped chancel. The simplicity of the herring-bone pattern distinguishable on the walls is typical of Early Romanesque decoration in Normandy.

Caudebec-en-Caux Pop. 2,500

This little town, only a few kilometres from St-Wandrille, looks back on an eventful history of alternating French and English rule. After submitting to Henri IV in 1592 it became prosperous, manufacturing gloves and hats. Henri called the church of *Notre-Dame* in the centre of Caudebec 'the most beautiful chapel in my kingdom'. Built in the Flamboyant style between 1425 and 1539, the church has a splendid 54-m-high tower, deeply recessed and richly decorated west doors, side chapels which have largely retained their original furnishings, and beautiful 16th c. stained-glass windows in which a luminous orange-gold colour stands out. The 13th c. Templars' House is now a museum of local history. Visitors to the *Musée de la Marine de Seine* will learn all sorts of interesting things about the navigation of the Seine, ships and fishing, and the ports and their maritime trade.

The Brotonne Forest is enclosed within a great bend in the Seine, at the head of which lies Caudebec. It is reached by way of the *Brotonne Bridge*. This once isolated area is no longer as peaceful as it was, but there are still many attractive spots to be found in the nature reserve, and several 'unofficial' sights such as the old baker's oven, the *Tour à Pain*, in *La Haye-de-Routot*, and the *Maison du Sabotier*, the clogmaker's house, where crafts once extinct can be found revived.

Back on the other side of the Seine the next stop, especially for those with an interest in French literature, will be Villequier.

In Villequier is the *Musée Victor Hugo*, in a villa formerly belonging to the Vacquerie family into which Hugo's beloved daughter Léopoldine married. She and her husband were drowned in the Seine in a boating accident in 1843, just six months after their marriage. The house contains many mementos.

The Château d'Etelan, the 15th c. village *church* and the *Maison Blanche* (an old hunting lodge) make a short stop in *St-Maurice-d'Etelan* worth while. The ravishingly beautiful Late Gothic château is, however, open to the public for only six weeks during the high season (enquire locally about opening times).

At Lillebonne are found the overgrown yet unmistakable tiers of a *Roman theatre*. There is also a small but attractive *museum of popular art*.

In Gruchet-le-Valasse some of the rooms in the old *Cistercian abbey* still preserve their medieval atmosphere and repay the detour.

Montivilliers is on the outskirts of Le Havre. The collegiate church of *St-Sauveur* effectively has two naves, the Romanesque earlier one and the Gothic one added by way of enlargement. It also has a massive central tower and some curious early sculptures in the south transept.

Le Havre Pop. 200,000

Being France's second largest port, the third largest in Europe and the most heavily damaged of all by the end of the Second World War, Le Havre has few pretensions to the picturesque. Even so the city is far more interesting than its reputation suggests. Nowhere else in Europe embraced what was then modernity as seriously and wholeheartedly as Le Havre did in its rebuilding.

Situated on the funnel-shaped estuary of the Seine, Le Havre is comparatively young. François I commissioned its construction in 1517 as a replacement for Harfleur further up the estuary, at that time the main port in the north but silting up badly. The strong fortifications – removed only in 1852 – meant that the English were able to land here only once, in 1562. In the Second World War, however, 80% of Le Havre was destroyed and the town, which between 1541 and 1543 had been enlarged by the Italian architect Bellarmato on a chessboard pattern, was 400 years later forced back to the drawing board. This time it re-emerged with the gigantic horizontal structures of Auguste Perret, the fanatical pioneer of reinforced concrete. The monumental and typically French *Avenue Foch* runs all the way from the town hall to the *Porte Océane* and the sea. The Avenue and the vast *Place de l'Hôtel de Ville*, with its correspondingly enormous town hall surmounted by an extremely austere concrete tower, lie within the new district created around the *Bassin du Commerce*. Accentuating the Bassin's role as focal point is the *Espace Oscar Niemeyer*, designed by the architect of Brazil's capital Brasilia. This square with its strange tower shapes constitutes the cultural centre of the town, including a large theatre.

Both the extremely modern-looking *Musée des Beaux-Arts André Malraux* by the harbour and the church of *St-Joseph* with its massively spacious interior and enormous (109 m) tower make you wonder whether the architecture of the post-war era has not perhaps sometimes lost its sense of human scale. Le Havre is worth seeing precisely because the question is seldom posed so clearly. On the other hand some would say that the Malraux Museum with its adjustable interior spaces is admirably functional. Among its many works of art, old and new, is an outstanding collection of paintings by the pre-Impressionist Eugène Boudin (1824–98).

From the museum it is an easy walk to the cathedral of *Notre-Dame* – an inspired mixture of a building, dating from about 1600 – and then to the lovely old house containing the *Musée de l'Ancien Havre* where the history of the city and its harbour is brought to life. In the eastern part of the city, towards Harfleur, is the *Abbaye de Graville*; the museum and church (partly Romanesque, with lovely capitals) provide a glimpse into the Middle Ages.

Whether you go on a tour of the harbour (information from the Tourist Office or the Centre Administratif du Port Autonome) or are satisfied with just the panoramic view from the *Fort de Ste-Adresse*, you are sure to be impressed by the curious monumentality of modern-day Le Havre.

Astoria, 13 Cours République, tel. 35 25 00 03; *France et Bourgogne*, 21 Cours République, tel. 35 25 40 34; *La Petite Auberge*, 32 Rue Ste-Adresse, tel. 35 46 27 32.

Harfleur, now part of greater Le Havre, is famous for its 83-m-high Gothic *church tower*. There is also a small *museum* in a charming half-timbered building which used to be the seamen's hospice.

Evreux to Bayeux

Evreux Pop. 48,600

Administrative centre of the Eure department

Once the main settlement of a Celtic tribe but falling to the Romans in 52 BC, Evreux became one of the most prosperous towns in Gaul. In the 5th c. it was made a bishopric and in 911 it was taken by the Normans. In the course of its chequered history Evreux has been destroyed at least half a dozen times, most recently by the Germans in 1940 and the Allies in 1944.

Begun in the 10th c. and continued in the 12th to 14th c., and then again in the 16th and 17th c., the cathedral of *Notre-Dame* shared in the town's fate. The war damage, though, has now been almost completely repaired. The variform exterior (note especially the 16th c. façade of the north transept) conceals a magnificently furnished interior. The Renaissance screens in the chapels are unrivalled, whilst the quality of the light filtering through the 14th c. windows adds to the beauty of the chancel.

The chancel of *St-Taurin* is also blessed with superb windows, but its greatest treasure is a High Gothic shrine, the silver-gilt *Châsse de St-Taurin*, in a chapel in the north transept. The 1.2-m-high and 1-m-long reliquary in the form of a miniature chapel contains the saint's bones and is one of the finest examples of the 13th c. goldsmith's

craft in France. It was modelled on the shrine from the Sainte-Chapelle in Paris, now sadly lost.

Also worth a visit is the museum in the *Ancien Evêché*, the former bishop's palace next to the cathedral. It includes sections on archaeology, local history and religious art. The *Tour de l'Horloge* (clock-tower) was one of the defence towers which guarded the town's main gate. A footpath now runs along what remains of the ramparts which encircled the town.

❌ *Normandy*, 3 Rue E. Feray, tel. 32 33 14 40; *France*, 29 Rue St-Thomas, tel. 32 39 09 25; *Auberge de Parville*, 4 km away in Parville, tel. 32 39 36 63.

Le Neubourg, about 25 km from Evreux, stands out against the surrounding *Plaine de Neubourg*. Its wide squares (designed to accommodate its markets) give the little town a spacious feel. A castle, the late medieval church of *Sts-Pierre-et-Paul* (with Baroque decoration in the chancel) and some handsome houses are all impressive.

Brionne, 15 km further on, has a pretty 14th to 15th c. church (*St-Martin*) and a *maison de Normandie*. The façade of the latter is typical: a lower storey with a geometric pattern in stone and brick, and a half-timbered upper storey. A fifteen-minute walk up to the 11th c. *keep* is amply rewarded by both the architecture of the square building and the view over the valley of the Risle.

Le Bec-Hellouin Abbey. It is hard to appreciate today just how important this abbey was in the Middle Ages. The old monastery buildings and the huge 15th c. church were demolished in the 19th c. leaving only a few column bases to give an indication of the original proportions. The *St-Nicolas Tower* is still standing, however, and there is also the *new abbey church* in what was once the magnificent refectory of the old monastery. The cloister, at the top of the massive grand staircase, was built in the mid-17th c.

Pont-Audemer. With a population of 10,200 this pretty town to the north-west of Le Bec-Hellouin has two churches, parts of both being old. *St-Ouen* has Late Gothic decoration in the nave and superb Renaissance stained-glass windows, while *St-Germain* dates from the 11th to 14th c. There are also a number of well-preserved half-timbered houses in the town centre.

Lisieux Pop. 25,800

After Lourdes this is the most famous and most visited of all the 'modern' pilgrim centres in France. Thérèse Martin — known as 'Little Teresa' to distinguish her from St Teresa of Avila, the 'great' Teresa who reformed the Carmelite Order — was allowed to enter the Carmelite Convent at Lisieux in 1888 when only fifteen years of age. This was despite the opposition of her father and the Church authorities and followed an audience with the Pope himself. She died there in 1897 after a short but saintly life. Little Teresa came to represent a model of patience, humility and religious faith for many Christians as a result of her autobiography *History of a Soul*. Her remains now lie in the *Chapelle du Carmel* in a crystal sarcophagus containing an effigy of the saint. A short but moving commentary on her life (also in English) is provided in the *Salle du Souvenir*, the reliquary chamber next to the chapel.

Les Buissonnets, St Teresa's childhood home (she was actually born in Alençon), has been meticulously preserved and is open to the public. Work on the huge 'Romanesque-Byzantine' *Basilique Ste-Thérèse* was begun in

Lisieux – Basilique Ste-Thérèse

1929, four years after her canonisation, and the building was consecrated in 1954. It must be one of the least successful works of religious architecture this century.

The (former) cathedral of *St-Pierre* – heart of the Lisieux diocese until the bishopric was abolished in 1801 – was built between 1170 and 1250. It is distinguished particularly by the splendidly articulated façade and by the arches in the nave. The central ambulatory chapel was remodelled in the 15th c. in pure Flamboyant style. Elsewhere in Lisieux be sure not to miss the Gold Chamber in the *Palais de Justice*, the old lawcourts. And in the *Musée du Vieux Lisieux* you can immerse yourself in the traditions of the Pays d'Auge, the region in which the town is situated.

Grand Hôtel Normandie, Rue au Char, tel. 31 62 16 05; *Coupe d'Or*, 49 Rue Pont-Mortain, tel. 31 31 16 84.

Pont-l'Evêque. A detour is necessary if you want to pay homage here at the 'home' of one of France's best-known cheeses. In contrast to Camembert it has been produced since the 13th c. and has remained rather exclusive, largely because of its price. Also in Pont-l'Evêque you will find the Late Gothic church of *St-Michel* and two town mansions, the *Hôtel Montpensier* and the *Hôtel de Brilly*, dating from the 17th and 18th c. respectively.

Crèvecœur-en-Auge. The village is roughly half-way between Lisieux and Caen. Its *Manoir de Crèvecœur* provides a delightful opportunity to visit a country estate dating back to the Middle Ages with a home-farm, barn, château, chapel and especially unusual dovecot. Housed in some of the half-timbered buildings is a petroleum

museum called the *Musée Schlumberger*, after the brothers from Alsace who were pioneers of petroleum research.

Caen Pop. 117,000
Administrative centre of the Calvados department

Caen owes its most precious architectural heritage, the Abbaye aux Hommes (a monastery) and the Abbaye aux Dames (a convent), to the marriage of William the Bastard, later 'the Conqueror', to Matilda of Flanders. Matilda at first rejected William because of his illegitimacy, but the love-struck duke abducted her from Lille and she eventually agreed to the marriage. However, the union was opposed by the Pope because the couple were cousins, and an order of excommunication was issued against them. The order could be lifted only by the building of two abbeys and four hospitals. After that Caen played the leading role in the affairs of Basse Normandie, as indeed it still does today. In 1944 the city was under siege for two months and in flames for eleven days; three-quarters of it was destroyed. It has recovered completely and its most important buildings have been restored.

 What to see
The *Memorial* (also called the *Musée de la Paix*), opened in 1988, is France's foremost and best war museum, or rather peace museum. It is situated just outside the city at the site of a German Second World War command headquarters (integrated into the museum). It has a completely plain façade with just one large opening in the centre. This entrance leads into an immense, utterly modern interior within which is a combination of traditional museum, audio-

visual displays, realistic reconstructions, memorials, and a super-cinema on whose wide screen can be seen the Allies landing and the Germans fighting their final battles. The museum also arranges temporary exhibitions on specific themes relating to the war years.

The *Abbaye aux Hommes* (Men's Abbey) comprises the Romanesque church of *St-Etienne* and the adjoining 18th c. monastery buildings. The two different styles harmonise surprisingly well. Built between 1066 and 1077, the church has a perfect Norman façade. Unadorned, but of compelling grandeur, it has three doorways, two rows of plain windows, and flanking towers with blind arcades. The spires were added in the Gothic period. Inside, the austerity of the nave gives way to an Early Gothic chancel. The tomb of the abbey's founder (below the lantern tower) was desecrated both in the Huguenot uprisings and during the Revolution. The apse with its three entirely different storeys is arguably more impressive from the outside than from within – you can see it best from the gardens of the monastery buildings. The latter, with their elegant staircases, magnificently carved woodwork and pleasingly proportioned halls, definitely warrant a visit. Although the buildings now house the *City Hall* some rooms are open to the public.

About half-way between the former abbey and the convent on the other side of Caen is the church of *St-Pierre*. It stands below William the Conqueror's *castle*, within whose massive ramparts are two museums and the medieval chapel of *St-Georges*. St-Pierre was built at the end of the Middle Ages with the aid of contributions from the city's wealthy townsfolk. It is crowned by what must be the most beautiful spire in the whole of Normandy (destroyed in the Second World War but subsequently

The Abbaye aux Hommes, Caen

rebuilt). The great marvel of St-Pierre, however, is its early 16th c. apse, whose exterior is exceptionally ornate and whose interior is like some stalactite-filled fantasy cave.

The *Musée des Beaux-Arts* in the castle grounds has sixteen rooms of 15th to 19th c. paintings, including some outstanding works by Flemish, Venetian and French artists. The museum also possesses an unusually fine collection of copper engravings. The *Musée de Normandie* in the former Governor's House includes displays in the form of thematic illustrations of life in Normandy.

The *Abbaye aux Dames*, founded by Queen Matilda, has suffered a certain amount of modification. The heavy balustrades on the towers, 18th c. replacements for the original spires, give this sister establishment to the Abbaye aux Hommes a somewhat squat appearance, and the middle section of the façade is not entirely in harmony with the lower storeys of the towers. The late 11th and 12th c. interior is however astonishingly pure, the articulation of the main nave being unusually attractive. The tomb of the royal founder can be seen in the chancel. The 11th c. crypt with its sixteen columns is perfectly preserved.

Paling in comparison with these great abbey churches are the late 17th c. Jesuit church of *Notre-Dame-de-la-Gloriette*, the rather unusual church of *St-Sauveur* (14th and 15th c.), and the Late Gothic church of *St-Jean*.

Many of Caen's secular buildings destroyed in the War have never been rebuilt. In the Rue St-Pierre, however, are some really lovely *half-timbered houses*, while the *Hôtel d'Escoville*, which has a delightful inner courtyard, conveys the full splendour of a wealthy Renaissance merchant's mansion.

✗ *Hôtel Moderne* with its restaurant *4 Vents*, 116 Bd Maréchal Leclerc, tel. 31 86 04 23; *Le Dauphin*, 29 Rue Gemare, tel. 31 86 22 26.

After visiting Caen take the Creully road for Bayeux, passing first through *Thaon* where there is a 12th c. Romanesque church and then on to Fontaine-Henry.

The Château de Fontaine-Henry, an absolutely glorious Renaissance building with an extraordinarily steep roof, is by far the most attractive château for many miles around. Its beautifully furnished rooms with some unusual paintings are open to view.

Bayeux Pop. 15,200

Celts, Romans, Saxons, Franks, Norsemen, English, Normans and finally the French have successively controlled Bayeux over the centuries. It was already a bishopric in the 5th c. and its history is closely intertwined with that of the dukes of Normandy (see page 16). Bayeux's two main sights are both major works of Norman art.

The world-famous Bayeux tapestry, the *Tapisserie de la Reine Mathilde*, is neither a woven tapestry nor, as its name might suggest, the work of Queen

The Château de Fontaine-Henry near Caen

The world-famous Bayeux Tapestry

Matilda. It is actually a kind of embroidered strip some 70 m long and 50 cm high, and was made in the 11th c., almost certainly in England. The fifty-eight scenes with Latin captions form a continuous picture sequence which provides an amazingly graphic portrayal of the Norman conquest of England. The tapestry was created by embroidering over pre-drawn lines, woollen threads being first laid over the areas to be covered and then stitched into place with wool of the same colour. The naturally dyed wool in shades of ochre, green, warm umber and muted red on the linen background gives the whole tapestry an extremely refined yet at the same time wonderfully fresh quality.

The *museum* built specially to house the tapestry stands only 100 m from the cathedral. In order to safeguard the colours only sparing use is made of light in the narrow, corridor-like room where visitors can walk the full length of the tapestry which is protected behind glass. The embroidery is a quite extraordinary rarity since similar textiles have been passed down to us only as fragments. The artistic quality is overwhelming and the importance of the historico-cultural details – of ships, tools, ceremonial, warfare, etc. – is con-

siderable. It is worth remembering, too, that this is the first ever edition, so to speak, of a comic strip – and it is just as gripping. Taped commentaries are available (also in English) and are definitely worth taking advantage of; the forty minutes simply fly by, even for children.

The façade and nave walls of the cathedral of *Notre-Dame*, Bayeux's second major attraction, are a combination of Norman Romanesque and Gothic elements (11th and 12th c.), the original Romanesque building having had to be restored after a fire. The two styles blend together very harmoniously. The 75-m towers of the façade are most imposing but the crossing-tower underwent neo-Gothic restoration at which time it was also raised. This should really be corrected since it distorts the proportions of the otherwise elegant building. The triple-naved Romanesque *crypt* is distinguished by its lovely capitals. The 12th c. *chapter-house*, abutting a side aisle, is beautifully articulated and has some delightful architectural sculptures. The cathedral *treasury* may also be visited.

Since Bayeux was spared in the Second World War the town retains considerable atmosphere. The Old Town is characterised by its half-timbered

The tower of La Madeleine, Verneuil-sur-Avre

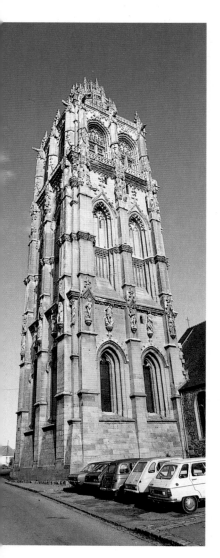

houses. Also of interest is the *Musée Baron Gérard* in the former Bishop's Palace. It has collections of early Italian and 18th and 19th c. French paintings together with porcelain and ceramics, tapestries and Normandy lace. The *Musée Mémorial de la Bataille de Normandie* on the edge of the town features photographs and films as well as tanks.

✕✕ *Brunville*, 9 Rue G. Duhomme, tel. 31 21 18 00; *Lion d'Or*, 71 Rue St-Jean, tel. 31 92 06 90.

East to west across southern Normandy

The old frontier on the Avre

The middle fortress of five on the River Avre which, from the 11th c., formed the defence line on the frontier between Normandy and France, *Verneuil-sur-Avre*, though French since 1205, then changed hands a number of times during the Hundred Years War. It is worth going there to see the ruins of the castle, its moat linked to the four other frontier fortifications by a sophisticated canal system fed by the River Iton. The two churches are also well worth seeing, *La Madeleine* on account of its 60-m high tower, built in the Flamboyant style at the end of the 15th c. and embellished by twenty-four statues, and which resembles the Butter Tower of Rouen Cathedral, and *Notre-Dame* (12th to 15th c.) which contains a large number of good-quality 12th to 17th c. wood carvings and sculptures, the earliest being a 12th to 13th c. painted wooden Madonna. The 35-m-high *Tour Grise* must be one of the most delightful of 12th c. round towers, and was part of a castle built by Henry I of England who founded the town.

Two famous women

Two notable women are associated with this particular area. The Comtesse de Ségur (1799–1874) was a Russian by birth. Her novels (for example *Les Malheurs de Sophie*), read widely till this century and not only in France, give a minutely detailed picture of the valley of the Risle. The little *Musée Ségur Rostopchine* in *Aube-sur-Risle* is devoted to the writer and her work.

The region's other famous woman, Alphonsine Plessis (1824–47), was much admired by Alexandre Dumas the Younger and was the model for his *Lady of the Camellias* whose fate – recorded in his novel (1848), his play (1852) and Verdi's *La Traviata* – was to touch the world. In *Gacé*, to the west of L'Aigle, there is a small museum dedicated to her (beyond St-Evroult Abbey which was famous in the 11th c. but is now in ruins).

The Pays d'Ouche

The barrenness of the Pays d'Ouche countryside along the upper course of the Risle encouraged the search for natural resources in the area in the early 19th c., which led to the discovery of iron and copper deposits in particular. The water power used to drive some fifty flour-mills situated along the banks of the river between St-Sulpice and Planches was further harnessed for metal-processing – copper-forges, naileries, and needle and wire production. There is still something to be seen of the mills and forges, but in L'Aigle and Rugles competition with the English meant that small-scale manufacture of pins and needles had to give way to larger undertakings.

Aube, Conches and La Ferrière. This same chapter in the region's industrial history is documented in a museum in *Aube-sur-Risle*. The furnaces and foundries of the area were once widely known, including those at *Conches-en-Ouche*, the main centre of the district, which today has scarcely 4,000 inhabitants but whose church, *Ste-Foy* (15th to 16th c.), boasts a lead spire (1851). The famous spire on Rouen Cathedral was also cast at Conches. *La Ferrière-sur-Risle*, with its 14th c. *market hall*, 16th c. *smithy* and 13th c. *church*, took its name from the iron ore which had already been uncovered here in Roman times.

Châteaux in the area. *Thevray Castle* (1489), not far from La Ferrière, is a rare combination of fortress and residence. Also worth a visit is the *Château de Beaumesnil*, a gem from the time of Louis XIII with an exceptionally ornate façade in brick and stone. The château, constructed around a central domed staircase between 1633 and 1640, was described as 'a dream in stone' by the Normandy writer La Varende in his novel *Nez-de-cuir*.

Le Perche

The old county of Perche, united with the French Crown in 1226, is now divided into *Le Perche Normand* and *Le Perche Gouët* (Île-de-France). It is an upland grass region across which run the *Collines du Perche*, bordered by three areas of forest. Even under Colbert, minister of finance to Louis XIV, these already enjoyed special protection against indiscriminate felling (the trees could only be cut down every 100 to 150 years).

Traditional butter-making

The forest around the small town of *Bellême* is exceptionally beautiful, as also is *Mortagne-au-Perche*, county town of the Normandy Perche and set on a low hill. Gate towers in both towns show they were once fortified.

From the 13th c., manor houses and even farms in the Perche were commonly fortified, some with keeps. The most typical are the *Manoir de Courboyer* (15th c.) to the east of Bellême and the *Manoir de la Vove* on the edge of the *Forêt de Réno-Valdieu*. Also typical are the châteaux with steeply pitched slate roofs, an example of which is the 16th c. *Château des Feugerets* south of Bellême.

The first 150 families to settle in Quebec after the founding by Richelieu of the Nouvelle France Trading Company originated from *Tourouvre* and *Mortagne*; this is an early example of that exodus from the countryside which continues even today in this principally agricultural area.

On the edge of the *Forêt du Perche* stands the *Abbaye de la Grande Trappe*, a monastery with a chequered history founded in 1140 on the site of an earlier votive church. It gave its name to the Trappist Order (a very strict branch of the Cistercians) which was established there in 1664 by the Abbot de Rancé. Today the monks live in a 19th c. building which combines neo-Gothic and neo-Romanesque elements. It is not open to the public.

The Percheron

The Perche is a land of horses. They have been bred here for centuries, and one particular strain has come to be known as the 'Percheron'. These black or grey animals with Arab blood were first in demand as post-horses, later being shipped to England and the USA as robust draught-horses for work on the land. Nowadays the breed is maintained, largely for nostalgic reasons, by only a few stud-farms. Among them is the National Stud at *Haras du Pin*, the oldest stud-farm in Normandy. Founded in 1665 by Colbert, it is administered from a château-like building designed by Mansart (1728) within a park laid out by Le Nôtre. Eight different breeds are kept here. From February to July eighty-two stallions ensure a supply of thoroughbred offspring for the stud as well as for its twenty-three branches. (Haras du Pin is open to visitors on Thursdays from May 19th to September 22nd. Entry is free, with informative half-hourly tours of the stables and the carriage collection. A horse-show with horse-racing is held on the first Sunday in August.)

Around Argentan

The *Pays d'Argentan*, dotted with many châteaux and manor houses (indicative of the former presence of an efficient feudal system), makes its living today from horses, farming and light industry.

Argentan itself lies in the centre of a large depression bordering the Dives valley. As a major crossroads inland from the Normandy coast it was largely destroyed in the Second World War, mainly following the Allied landings and the Battle of Falaise.

There are two restored churches, *St-Germain* (begun in 1410) and *St-Martin*. The latter was originally one of the earliest monuments to the Christianisation of these parts by St Martin of Tours; a church was constructed here in the 4th c., over a heathen temple. Both churches bear witness to the transition from Late Gothic to Renaissance (see especially the Flamboyant north porch of St-Germain). The *Tour Marguerite* (15th c.) with its machicolations is one remnant of the town's former fortifications while of the 14th c. *castle* only three towers are still standing. It was in the nearby Capuchin monastery *(Lycée Méceray)* that Adrien de Corday was taken prisoner after his daughter Charlotte's assassination of the Revolutionary Jean-Paul Marat in 1793. The nuns of the Benedictine *abbey* (restored in 1958) are the custodians of the secret of Argentan lace *(point d'Argentan)*, a skill they practise using old patterns rediscovered in 1864 in the town's hospice. (The abbey is open to visitors daily, 2.30–6 pm, excluding Sundays and public holidays.)

The châteaux. Buildings in this tract of countryside watered by the Orne (and known also as the *Hièmois* or the *Pays d'Exmes*) are all built of brick and quarried limestone, be they farmhouses, castles or anything else. In the north of the area more limestone is used in the rather severe, flat façades, in the south more brick. The châteaux typically have steep slate roofs and pointed pepper-pot turrets, like those of the *Château d'O*, for instance, which was built by François d'O, the unfortunate finance minister first of Henri III and then of Henri IV. D'O lived in even grander style than the King himself according to Sully, who finally set the State finances to rights (though not those of d'O who died heavily in debt).

A little to the north, on the D 26, the *Château de Médavy* (11th c.), protected by mighty towers and moats, guarded the Orne crossing. Further west is the 18th c. *Château de Sassy* with its French-style garden, richly endowed library, and chapel which contains the Gothic altar from the abbey of St Bavo in Ghent. Like the Château d'O it also has a very pleasing *dovecot*, though in these parts this particular status symbol is often replaced by an ornamental pigeon-hole in the wall of the house. The château at *Le-Bourg-St-Léonard* which was built only twenty-two years before the French Revolution is now a museum of pre-Revolutionary times.

Beyond the old Merovingian town of *Exmes*, now just a tiny place, and past the beautifully situated *Manoir d'Argentelles*, a half-timbered Renaissance building, the road leads to the 12th c. *Chambois Castle* with its four corner towers. From the Romanesque church here you can also catch a glimpse of a Gothic bath-house. On August 21st 1944, in the bloody Battle of Chambois which cost more than 10,000 lives, the Allied forces managed to close the *Poche de Falaise*. The German troops were forced to surrender and so the Battle of Normandy was ended.

Sées Pop. 5,000

The cathedral of *Notre-Dame* towers over the little town of Sées, as it has done since the Middle Ages. A bishopric since the 4th c. (one of the oldest in Normandy), Sées was ravaged by the Vikings in the 9th c. In the 11th c. the cathedral was accidentally set alight by the bishop of Bellême in the course of a man-hunt, his quarry having taken refuge there. The present building was erected between 1278 and 1292 and is one of the finest examples of Normandy Gothic. The 70-m towers are visible for miles around. The interior, with its second gallery above the triforium and its small windows (some of which date from the 14th and 15th c.), is reminiscent of the cathedral at Bayeux. Also noteworthy is the medieval *Notre-Dame* figure facing the altar. The town has two other churches dedicated to Mary: *Notre-Dame de la Place* which has twelve 16th c. bas-reliefs, and *Notre-Dame du Vivier* from which there is a particularly lovely view of the cathedral. The Bishop's Palace dates from 1778. The *Museum of Religious Art* contains some fine examples of sacred sculpture from the last six centuries as well as an ivory comb which belonged to Thomas à Becket, Henry II's chancellor and later Archbishop of Canterbury, who went into exile in France in 1164. After an apparent reconciliation with Henry he returned to Canterbury where he was murdered in 1170. Henry finally received absolution for this crime at Avranches Cathedral.

Alençon Pop. 32,500

Two duchesses, both named Marguerite, have left their imprint on this town built on the banks of the River Sarthe. The first duchess, Marguerite de Lorraine, was by all accounts a woman whose piety was matched only by her gaiety. The church of *St-Léonard*, which stands amidst 15th and 16th c. houses in the old district of the same name, was begun by her husband René, but it was Marguerite who completed it with an elegant Late Gothic nave and doorway in the Flamboyant style. Also in this style is the very ornate three-gabled porch of *Notre-Dame* designed for the Duchess by Jean Lemoine. The Renaissance windows in this church are exceptionally fine examples of the period.

Alençon's second important duchess, Marguerite de Valois-Angoulême, kept sophisticated court with her husband Charles at the *Maison d'Ozé* (1450), a horseshoe-shaped palace which stands right next to Notre-Dame and which dates from the Middle Ages and Renaissance.

St Teresa of Lisieux was born on January 2nd 1873 at no. 50 Rue St Blaise. You can find her birthplace not far from the *Hôtel de Guise* (a superb Louis XIII building of 1630) and the *Drapers' Hall* (1827).

Beyond the circular *Halle au Blé* (Corn Exchange, 1812–65) you come to what remains of the late 14th c. *castle* with its massive towers (now used as a prison), and also to the *town hall* (1783). An exceptionally interesting museum has been created in the former *Jesuit college* (1620). This *Musée des Beaux Arts* possesses a number of good paintings from the 15th c. to the present day, an unusual collection from Cambodia, an exhibition of lace, and a library which once belonged to Valdieu Abbey (founded in 1170 but destroyed during the Revolution) containing incunabula and early editions of the Bible, for example a 1478 edition from Nuremberg.

Hôtel de la Gare, 50 Av Wilson, tel. 33 29 03 93. *Petit Vatel*, 72 Place du Cdt. Desmeulles, tel. 33 26 23 78.

Alençon lace

The old ducal town of Alençon made its name from the 'Queen of lace', the needlepoint produced here which evolved from hemstitching and open-work techniques. Until the 17th c. people had had to buy this sort of lace in Venice so that more money was finding its way to the 'city on the lagoons' than was good for the French Exchequer. It was for this reason that Colbert, the pioneer under Louis XIV of state intervention in the economy, had Venetian lacemakers brought to Alençon in 1650. The local women mastered the craft completely. It used to take a needlewoman four hours of work to make just one square centimetre of *Point d'Alençon*, 'French lace'. She would have to have trained for a full seven years and even then, so jealously guarded was the secret, would never have been allowed to learn all the steps used in the lacemaking process. The French Revolution, however, spelled the end of such luxuries. Today the art of lacemaking is demonstrated in the *Atelier-Conservatoire du Point d'Alençon* (Rue du Pont-Neuf, daily except Sun. and Mon. from April 15th to September 15th). In addition there is a lace section in the *Musée des Beaux-Arts*. The *Atelier National du Point d'Alençon* in the old Jesuit college (Îlot Charles Aveline) is the former School of Lacemaking.

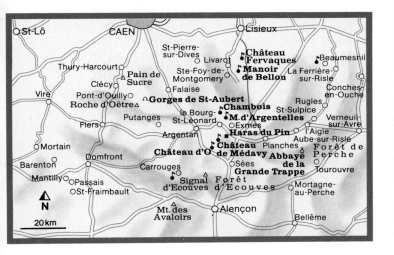

The green frontier of southern Normandy

In 1975 the belt of green forest between Alençon and Mortain which forms the southern frontier of Normandy was turned into a vast 234,000-hectare regional park covering 152 different districts in four *départements*. This heterogeneous natural museum is not intended simply to promote tourism; it is also designed to stimulate the area's farming, forestry and handicrafts. It is administered from the old prebendary's house at Château de Carrouges (*Maison du Parc Naturel Régional Normandie-Maine*, open daily except Sat. and Sun., 8.30 am–12.30 pm and 1.30–5.30 pm). Here you can obtain information on walking and other sports as well as special events, and also on the particular spots worth visiting in the area – the game-rich *Forêt d'Ecouves*, for example, with the joint highest summit in Normandy, Signal d'Ecouves (417 m), and the *Chapelle de Goult*, its entrance embellished by six 12th c. capitals decorated with animal and hunting scenes. Then there is the *Château de Carrouges* itself with its woods and park and its austere and complex castle buildings (14th c. onwards) in brick and granite, built around an inner courtyard and all encircled by a moat. The interior is sumptuously decorated in the styles of Louis XIII to Louis XVI. Or again there are the gushing waters of the thermal spring at *Bagnoles-de-l'Orne* (the spa architecture dates from about 1900). Bagnoles is situated in a clearing in the forest, as are many of the villages here, their houses half-timbered or of dry quarry-stone.

It is this area too which is thought to have been one source of the Celtic legend of Lancelot, knight of the Round Table, and his love for Guinevere, wife of King Arthur. Indeed Arthur is supposed to have disappeared in the *Fosse Arthour*, a gorge on the River Sonce – though he is also said to be buried in England. It was while Chrétien de Troyes was at the court of the beautiful Queen Eleanor of Aquitaine (who apparently liked to spend time at Domfront) that he is believed to have been inspired by the legend to write his famous epic poem.

Domfront, a little place known since 540, has the remains of an 11th c. castle in addition to its 11th c. church of *Notre-Dame-sur-l'Eau*, four bays of which were demolished in 1836 to make way for the Mortain road. A detour off that road leads to the *Abbaye de Lonlay*, a Benedictine monastery where there is a Romanesque-Gothic church (with interesting limestone capitals) and the remains of a chapter-house.

Through Barenton, Mantilly, Passais and on as far as St-Fraimbault runs the so-called *Route de la Poire* taking you into perry country. This is the home of *cidre de poire* which *cidre de pomme* (cider) threatens nowadays to replace.

The Normandy Bocage

Bocage is to be found everywhere in France where hedges of trees or shrubs growing on raised earth banks enclose fields and meadows. Typically villages and towns are few and far between; instead farmsteads lie widely scattered, as indeed they do in the Normandy Bocage, the westerly tract which extends from the Forêt d'Ecouves through the Suisse Normande to the borders of the Cotentin peninsula and the Bessin (the coastal area to the north of St-Lô). Guy de Maupassant described it in his novel *Notre Cœur* (1890) as a 'rolling landscape with blond cattle'. It is not a very fertile area and has few natural resources other than its rocky substrata of granite and slate from which the houses here are made and which, by preventing the ground water from seeping away, create marshlands covered with moss and rushes. The people make a living from dairy farming and by breeding cattle and horses.

St-Lô to the Route du Fromage

St-Lô, pop. 24,800, once had the sad nickname of 'Capital of the Ruins' when only the towers of the church of *Notre-Dame* (13th to 17th c.) and a few houses had been left standing after bombing in 1944. Today life in the rebuilt town has once again taken up the threads of its historic pattern with a cattle market held every month and a stud-farm for race-horses and thoroughbreds *(Haras de St-Lô)*. Among other things which should not be missed in the *Musée des Beaux-Arts* are eight 16th c. tapestries *(Tapisseries de Gorebaut et Macée)* idealising rural life at the time of Henri IV.

Vire, pop. 13,800. The town is perched on a hill around which the River Vire carves out one of its many bends.

Cattle in the cider orchard

Amongst the town's attractions are a fine clock-tower *(Tour de l'Horloge)*, remains of the fortifications (the *donjon*, a rather unusual square keep) and a *museum* devoted to local history and life in the Bocage. The Vire area also has its own gastronomic speciality, smoked *andouille* (see page 21).

Mortain, pop. 3,000, takes its name from the Moorish legions who in Roman times guarded the Brittany border. It has a particularly delightful setting on a crag overlooking the little River Cance, which here tumbles down over the rocks in two waterfalls known as the Petite and Grande *Cascades* (the latter almost 35 m high) before flowing on to the Cistercian *Abbaye Blanche* with its old chapter-house, cloister and chapel.

Flers, pop. 19,400, is surrounded by lakes and ponds. Like Mortain it was a centre of royalist resistance at the time of the French Revolution. Chief among its sights are the *castle* (16th to 18th c.) and the *Musée du Bocage Normand* housed within it and full of interesting local history.

Falaise pop, 8,800. No town surely could be a more fitting symbol of Norman resilience than Falaise. It was here in 1028 that Arlette, beautiful daughter of a local tanner, bore Robert the Magnificent (also called *le Diable*, the Devil) an illegitimate child, William the Bastard. In the event William turned out to be Robert's only son and when only seven years old succeeded to his father's burdensome inheritance, eventually to triumph against all the odds. It was here also in our own time – in August 1944 – that British and American troops encircled the German forces in what became known as the 'Falaise Pocket' *(la poche de Falaise)*, forcing them to capitulate.

You can still look down from Robert's *castle* high on the rock above the River Ante, just as the Duke must once have looked down, to the spot where, returning from the hunt, he was enchanted by the sight of Arlette as she washed clothes in the stream. What makes the full story of this unpromising liaison so pleasing is that the otherwise irresponsible Duke did not entirely abandon his loved one but married her off instead to the Vicomte de Conterville to whom she later bore William the Conqueror's two very influential half-brothers, Odo of Bayeux and Robert of Mortain.

At the castle you can visit the chapel and three of the original fifteen towers as well as the covered battlements (12th to 14th c.). The town behind it has been rebuilt together with its three churches: the part-Romanesque, part-Gothic *St-Gervais* with its light chancel wreathed in chapels, *La Trinité*, richly refurnished by its faithful, with a beautiful Renaissance porch, and the largely Gothic *Notre-Dame-de-Guibray* with its remarkable 18th c. Assumption group. Falaise used also to be known for its market of which the *arcades* in the Rue de Trun are relics.

St-Pierre-sur-Dives, pop. 4,500. On the way here you can make various detours, for example to the *Brèche au Diable* (Devil's Gap), a natural beauty spot, the Iron Age necropolis (700–450 BC) at *Mont-Joly*, and the ore workings at *Soumont-St-Quentin* (where there is a small museum), as well as to various châteaux and country estates (e.g. *Torps*). St-Pierre itself has one of the best-preserved abbeys in Normandy, with an enclosed courtyard and cloister. The well-proportioned church dates from the 13th c. and has an unusual lantern tower (also 13th c.) above the crossing; the south tower is Romanesque and the tall windows are 16th c. Inside the church is the tomb of the Comtesse Lesceline who founded the abbey in the 11th c. Be sure not to miss the superb 13th c. *enamelled tile floor* in the chapter-house, early testimony to the widespread use of ceramics here. The 11th to 12th c. *halles* (covered market) fell victim to the bombing in 1944 but have since been faithfully reconstructed (key at the *Café du Marché*). Most of the châteaux in the neighbourhood – for example the *Château de Vendeuvre* and the *Château de Canon* – are open to the public.

The abbey at St-Pierre still maintains the traditions of another Normandy art, cheese-making, and there is a *museum* on the subject in the east wing. Boxes for packing the highly seasoned Normandy cheeses are also manufactured in the town.

Livarot, only 16 km east of St-Pierre, is another small town which anyone setting out to follow the so-called *Route du Fromage* (maps available from the tourist office) will quickly come across. The town produces its own strongly flavoured cheese. In between stops at the various cheese cellars along the Route the observant visitor will also notice some interesting churches (the 16th c. *St-Martin-du-Mesnil-Oury*, for example),

The Manoir de Bellou near Livarot

equally interesting castles (such as the Renaissance *Château Fervaques*, where the diplomat and author Chateaubriand liked to stay), and country estates (the *Manoir de Bellou* and the *Manoir de Chiffretot*).

In Lisores is found a *Fernand Léger Museum* (open daily except Wed.), established in memory of the Argentan-born painter by his wife Nadia. The huge mosaic on the barn will tell you when you are there. Léger also made stained-glass windows for a *chapel* nearby.

The Suisse Normande

The Suisse Normande between Thury-Harcourt and Putanges (where Mont Pinçon, the highest hill in Calvados,

reaches all of 365 m) flaunts not so much its heights as the beautiful *valley of the Orne* and its tributaries which wind their way through chalk and granite cliffs. This is excursion country for the people of Caen (only 26 km away) and the destination of ramblers, hill-walkers, anglers and canoeists.

Between *Clécy* and *Putanges* lie three particular beauty spots – the *Pain de Sucre* (a small hill with a much acclaimed view), the *Roche d'Oëtre* near *Pont-d'Ouilly*, which rises 120 m above the rocky valley of the Rouvre, and the *Gorges de St-Aubert*, a series of gorges carved by the Orne.

In between are various manors and châteaux. Near Clécy are the ruined

The River Orne winds through its beautiful valley

castle of *La Pommeraye*, the 16th c. *Manoir de Placy* where there is a pottery and faience museum, and *Pontécoulant Château*, set in a park with ancient trees and housing the *Musée du Département* (mainly 16th to 18th c. furniture). There is much to see around Putanges as well, including the 16th c. *Château de Crèvecœur* (flanked by two large watch-towers), *Repas* Castle which dates from around 1615 and stands in

flat, open country encircled by water, and *Rabodanges* Castle which is constructed in the dark slate of the region and is not far from Rabodanges dam or from the ruined *Moulin de la Jalousie*.

The villages of the Suisse Normande were largely destroyed in the decisive battle for Falaise in 1944. Since then the 11th c. castle at *Thury-Harcourt*, the seat of a minor Norman duchy, has remained in ruins.

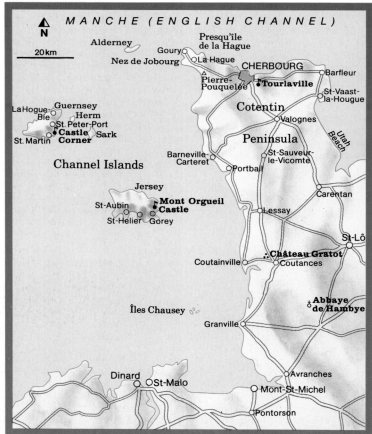

The Cotentin peninsula and Mont-St-Michel

The Cotentin peninsula, which 'crowns' north-west Normandy and extends southwards as far as Mont-St-Michel, is geologically a part of Brittany. The landscape of its northern coast is also similar to that of its western neighbour, and in many places (as at La Hague) is even wilder. The Cotentin's highest hill rises no higher than 183 m; it is a region of gently rolling countryside with steep cliffs along its northern coast. La Hague at its north-western tip has been brought to public attention by its nuclear reprocessing plant – publicity which the Cotentin could well have done without since its lovely countryside has always been something of a well-kept holiday secret. It is certainly worth making a special journey to see the peninsula and even worth spending a whole holiday there. You will discover lovely towns with outstanding cathedrals, an unspoilt landscape free as yet from large-scale invasion by tourists, rugged beaches, the Channel Islands on the doorstep, the opportunity to indulge in every kind of watersport, and in effect a separate world, lapped on three sides by the sea and on a scale you can easily take in. The Cotentin is more authentically and more starkly 'Nordic' than anywhere else in France.

Northwards to the Val-de-Saire

The bulge at the north-east tip of the Cotentin peninsula, through which flows the River Saire, is known as the Val-de-Saire. This very rewarding part of the east Cotentin is reached either by the coast road or from further inland via Valognes. Practically all the way along the coast, dunes separate the road from the sea. Utah Beach, starting point for the drive up the coast, keeps alive memories of the Allied landing. One-time German bunkers have been turned into memorials and museums.

Carentan is where the inland route to the Val-de-Saire begins. Its large church of *Notre-Dame* spans three centuries of Gothic style. The late south side is strikingly elegant and the spire dominates the town.

Valognes is the first port of call *en route*. One or two mansions – the 18th c. *Hôtel de Beaumont* in particular, with its extensive façade and its park – have survived to give just a glimpse of the former aristocratic splendours of the town, which sadly was otherwise largely destroyed in 1944. The *Musée Régional du Cidre* introduces visitors to the intricacies and traditions involved in making Normandy's famous cider.

 Haut Gallion, Route de Cherbourg, tel. 33 40 40 00.

St-Vaast-la-Hougue is a pretty fishing village and seaside resort and a good starting point for a drive through the lovely scenery of the east Cotentin. This area of squat granite houses and almost subtropical vegetation has a quite special charm.

Barfleur with its attractive quayside has an 18th c. *church* with a Late Romanesque tower. A few kilometres further on, however, is an even more exciting tower, the 71-m-high *Phare de la Pointe de Barfleur*. It is one of the highest lighthouses in France and offers an overwhelming panorama.

Cherbourg Pop. 90,000

Cherbourg has been fought over ever since the arrival of the Celts. In the Second World War it was a fortress of the Atlantic Wall and heavily bombed by the Allies. Today it is a passenger and commercial port of considerable though decreasing importance. Besides museums of natural and maritime history and a museum of the Second World War, Cherbourg also has the *Musée Thomas Henry* which possesses some good paintings by great masters including Lippi, Murillo and Chardin. Tropical plants thrive in the *Parc Emmanuel Liais*, thanks to the influence of the Gulf Stream. The church of the Holy Trinity or *Basilique Ste-Trinité*, first built about 1055, rebuilt in the 15th c. and restored again in the 19th c., has some very fine items among its furnishings. At the *Abbaye du Vœu* (founded by Queen Matilda in 1145) some of the older parts survive, in particular the south wing with the chapter-house and refectory.

 Mercure, Gare Maritime, tel. 33 44 01 11.

Tourlaville and the Allée Couverte. Standing in a magnificent park just to the east of Cherbourg is the Renaissance *Château de Tourlaville*, the grounds of which are open to the public. The *Allée Couverte*, a double line of megalithic stones lying further east still, is thought to be a communal grave from about 2000 BC.

The west side of the Cotentin
The Nez de Jobourg and environs. Beyond Cherbourg the drive westwards takes you round the north-east coast of the La Hague peninsula – from where there are stupendous views out to sea – until the little harbour of *Goury* and the *Nez de Jobourg*, the scenic highpoint of the journey, are reached. At *Pierre-Pouquelée* there is the opportunity for a final look back at the cliffs of the Nez before you head south down the west coast.

Barneville-Carteret, which is really two towns that have merged and which

also takes in *Barneville-Plage*, is easily the most well-known place on the peninsula's west coast. Of the two Carteret is the more elegant, Barneville being touchingly modest in comparison. It does however have a Romanesque *church* with some extremely interesting early capitals decorated with animal and plant motifs. There are delightfully refreshing walks along the beach and the cliffs.

 Les Isles, tel. 33 04 90 76; *L'Hermitage-Maison Duhamel*, tel. 33 04 96 29.

Portbail makes an impressive picture with its Romanesque *fortified church* by the harbour. Both Portbail and Carteret are popular points from which to cross to the Channel Islands.

Another very worthwhile excursion from Portbail takes you into the interior of the Cotentin peninsula.

St-Sauveur-le-Vicomte has a *castle museum* dedicated to the writer Barbey d'Aurevilly, who was born in the town, and a *church* with a Gothic transept and fine statues.

Due south of here is Lessay, which is also well worth a visit.

Lessay has a Romanesque *abbey* dating from the 11th c. The terrible destruction wrought upon it in 1944 is no longer evident and it must rank as a masterpiece of restoration and reconstruction. The clean lines of its Romanesque architecture, the two tiers of windows in the apse, the seven wide-arched bays of the nave and the deeply recessed gallery running all round the building, together with the restrained decoration, all contribute to the character of this flawless Benedictine church. Assuming it has been correctly dated to the 11th c., this is the very earliest church anywhere with groined vaulting.

(Some art historians, it should be said, consider it to be 12th c.)

The Lessay horse and dog fair held in September proudly refers to itself as 'one thousand years old'. This *Foire de la Ste-Croix* is also a full-blown popular festival.

Around Coutances

Château de Gratot. The château stands a little way off the road a few kilometres from Coutances, its four different towers making it quite impossible to miss. Its construction spanned five centuries, from the 14th to the 18th. Impeccably restored, it is now one of the countless venues in Normandy for summer concerts and theatre.

Coutances, pop. 13,400, is situated on a hill and dominated by the marvellous cathedral of *Notre-Dame*, a visit to which is an absolute must for anyone with an interest in art. The church was built in the 11th c. and burnt down in 1218, only to arise anew on the Romanesque remains, this time in Gothic style. The magnificently executed 78-m towers of the façade with their octagonal spires create an effect of soaring verticality. Inside, the nave and transept reveal an equal command of proportion and clever articulation. The lantern tower is one of the loveliest in Normandy. The oldest windows in the cathedral, dated to the 13th c., shine into the north transept, whilst gracing the south transept a 14th c. window of the Last Judgement. Coutances's church of *St-Pierre* also has a crossing-tower to be proud of, in this case a Renaissance tower which becomes increasingly ornate towards the top.

Coutainville, a seaside resort on the coast near Coutances, has a beach of fine sand and provides every aquatic activity a holidaymaker could wish for.

Abbaye de Hambye. The ruins of this abbey lie south-east of Coutances and include a Romanesque nave, two-storeyed crossing-tower, Gothic chancel and monastic buildings.

Granville Pop. 15,000

Granville is both seaside resort and commercial port. It is spread out below a rock on which stands the upper (old) town, still encircled by its ramparts — there is a splendid view from the *Place de l'Isthme*. The church of *Notre-Dame* (Late Gothic in part), the *Musée du Vieux Granville* which documents the town's history, the *lighthouse* and the *aquarium* all go to make a stay here thoroughly enjoyable. So does a day trip to the *Îles Chausey* some 12 km offshore, a granite archipelago comprising fifty islands and islets, the main one of which, *La Grande Île*, is 2 km long and 700 m wide. The fort, the castle, the fishermen's chapel and the lighthouse are the main points of interest on a walk round the island.

 Normandy-Chaumière, 20 Rue Dr Paul Poirier, tel. 33 50 01 71.

From Avranches to the journey's end

Avranches offers the visitor something by way of a foretaste of Mont-St-Michel. The abbey's famous collection of 8th to 15th c. manuscripts is on display in the *Musée de l'Avranchin*. From the *Jardin des Plantes* (botanical gardens) there is a much vaunted view of the Holy Mount.

 Auberge St-Michel, 7 Place Général Patton, tel. 33 58 01 98.

Pontorson. Here there is yet another church worth seeing, a 12th c. Gothic *hall church* with dark, austere façade. It was founded by William the Conqueror after he had survived the menacing quicksands of the River Couesnon during a campaign against the Bretons.

Mont-St-Michel

 Montgomery, Rue Couesnon, tel. 33 60 00 09.

Mont-St-Michel

Solitude and tranquillity can hardly be expected in a place visited by a million tourists and pilgrims every year. Even so, the abbey – whose astonishing Gothic buildings have led to its being called 'La Merveille de l'Occident' (the Wonder of the West) – creates a truly incomparable effect on top of its 80-m-high granite peak, to which the little town clings below. Soaring audaciously upwards, the Mount is encircled by the sea and can be approached only via a single causeway, a fact which seems to have had little effect in holding back the throng. Quite the reverse indeed: the barrier of the tides has served only to emphasise the spiritual independence of this island, joined to the mainland by so tenuous a thread. The stupendously high tides towards the vernal equinox, at the beginning of May, and again around the feast of St Michael (celebrated on

the nearest Sunday to September 29th) transform Mont-St-Michel into a floating holy city, one of the great images of Christianity. This is not just another 'sight' to be photographed and ticked off the list. All the piety and conviction of the Middle Ages are captured in microcosm on this rocky isle.

With its blue slate roofs, its limestone and its granite, high above the blue-green sea, now seeming to shimmer in the strong sunlight, now hunched under a veil of drizzle, or even rising above the elements, Mont-St-Michel transcends all the vagaries of the weather, just as it transcends all attempts to commercialise it. To appreciate its outline the better, try to imagine that its buildings are transparent so you can 'see' the flat-topped cone of rock beneath. On its north-west side the Mount is guarded by inaccessible rocks. To the east and south is a protective wall fortified by a series of towers. Within the wall the little town pushes up to a height of 50 m, at which point it gives way to the soaring monastery buildings. Try to visualise the

Mount itself as terraced below the platform supporting the abbey church with its tall spire and chancel. The various storeys of the abbey complex – the crypts and passages hidden from the outside behind massive buttressing walls, and above them the actual three-storeyed abbey building whose famous cloister is its crowning glory – stand one on top of another as though built on a flight of steps.

 History

In 708, after the Archangel Michael had appeared to him, Aubert, Bishop of Avranches, built an oratory on the Mount, which had been inhabited by monks since the 6th c. As the cult of St Michael spread, the oratory was replaced by a Carolingian abbey. In time a great complex of fortified abbey buildings arose taking in the whole of the Mount – so well protected that no one ever succeeded in capturing it. Even during the Hundred Years War pilgrims continued to make the perilous trip across the bay, bringing back souvenirs in the form of images of St Michael and lead ampoules filled with sand. Construction of the abbey buildings continued from the 11th to the 16th c. (the earlier structure had been a Benedictine house since 966). During the French Revolution, however, the monastery was dissolved and the abbey degraded; until 1863 it served as a state prison. It was returned to the monks two years later.

The nave and transept of the church were built in the 11th and early 12th c. The chancel is Late Gothic, and beneath it the earlier Carolingian church forms the crypt. After a collapse, which left the nave shortened, a Baroque façade was constructed. The exceptionally fine Gothic cloisters were completed in 1228.

 A tour of the abbey

The little town (which has a population of about 100) is entered through the *Porte du Roi*. Once in the *Grande Rue* with its charming old houses, go past (or pay a visit to) the heavily restored but welcoming parish church, and then follow the road as it winds up to the abbey. Here you must join one of the official tours, available in different languages and led by extremely knowledgeable guides. The earlier you arrive the smaller your group will be and the more compelling your encounter with the abbey (much the best time is around 9 am).

The round tour starts in the Romanesque-Gothic abbey church and first leads down to the *Crypte des Gros Piliers* and adjoining chambers cut in the rock. Next you pass through a pre-Carolingian inner chapel before arriving in the three-storeyed Gothic *Merveille abbey building* on the north side. The outer face of the building – the great wall supported by gigantic buttresses, and the stabilising influence, as it were, in the whole complicated picture – gives no indication of the elegance of the rooms within. Here on one level are the cloister and refectory, below them the Guests' Hall and the four-aisled Knights' Hall, and lower still the Almonry and the Pilgrims' Hall – now a reception area and bookshop. Each of these vast halls is in its own individual way a shining example of Gothic architecture.

Leaving by the Almonry go out on to the ramparts for some superb views. You can walk through the abbey *gardens* or, if the tide is right, you might decide to take a boat trip round the island.

 Terrasses Poulard, tel. 33 60 14 09.

Useful things to know

Before you go
When to go

Anyone who loves apple blossom should go to Normandy, and especially to Calvados, in April or May. With sea temperatures rarely exceeding 68°F/20°C, on the other hand, June to mid-August is the best time for bathing enthusiasts, though August coincides with the peak of the French holiday season. Hotels and other holiday facilities on the coast will tend to close down from the end of August.

If you have an interest in art and architecture, though, and are travelling independently, you can just as well visit other parts of the region any time between March and October.

Insurance

You are strongly advised to take out holiday insurance, including cover against medical expenses.

As a member of the EC France has a reciprocal agreement with other EC countries, under which free medical treatment can be obtained for those entitled to it in their own country. To obtain this benefit a UK national has to be in possession of form E111, obtainable from the DSS; an application form is available from the DSS or at main post offices.

Anyone travelling by car should arrange comprehensive insurance cover for the duration of the holiday.

Getting to Normandy

By sea: For British visitors Normandy is easily reached by ferry from the Channel ports: Dover/Folkestone–Calais/Boulogne, Newhaven–Dieppe, Portsmouth–Le Havre and Portsmouth–Cherbourg are equally good options, depending on where you are heading for in Normandy.

By air: All the major international airlines of course fly to Paris, but there are also airports at a number of major towns and cities in Normandy itself, for example at Rouen, Le Havre and Caen, which are serviced by both foreign and French carriers. The latter will be particularly useful if you wish to visit Normandy from Paris or other French cities. Ask your travel agent for details.

By rail: There is a good rail network within Normandy, and between Paris and Normandy. Trains for central and most northern towns leave Paris from the Gare St-Lazare; those for the southern towns leave from the Gare Montparnasse.

Passport and customs regulations

No visa required by British or US visitors staying under three months. British tourists need a valid standard passport or British Visitor's Passport.

Personal belongings of people entering the country are not subject to duty. These include still and video cameras, tape recorders, portable radios, telescopes and binoculars, portable typewriters and the usual camping equipment. In addition, EC residents may bring in (duty paid) 300 cigarettes (or 75 cigars or 400 g tobacco), 5 litres of wine and 1.5 litres of spirits over 22% (3 litres under 22%).

EC residents may take into or bring back from France duty free 200 cigarettes or 50 cigars or 250 g tobacco, 1 litre of spirits over 22% (2 litres under 22%) and 2 litres of wine.

Non-EC visitors should check allowances with their travel agent.

During your stay

Currency

The monetary unit in France is the French franc (F), equivalent to 100 centimes (c). Currently in circulation are coins up to the value of 10 F as well as banknotes in denominations of 10, 20, 50, 100 and 500 F. Exchange rates are subject to fluctuation and should be checked in the national press or at banks.

There are no restrictions on the import of foreign currency into France. All French banks, bureaux de change and most hotels will cash Eurocheques.

Credit cards are in fairly common use; most hotels, restaurants and petrol stations and many shops will accept the major ones. However, it is safest to carry a supply of cash with you against the possibility of their not being accepted.

Electricity

220 v/50 Hz AC. French sockets do not normally take the standard UK or US plug; a Continental adaptor (obtainable from electrical dealers) will almost certainly be necessary.

Hotel and hôtel

In French 'hôtel' means both a hotel in the English sense of the word and also a grand private residence or town mansion. In France the town hall is called the *hôtel de ville*, while *hôtel-Dieu* – literally 'House of God' – means a hospital (usually long established).

Opening times and entrance fees

Opening times vary a great deal. Many museums are shut on Mondays, others on Tuesdays. Many of the sights are open only in summer, some only in August or on one or two days a week (especially privately owned châteaux).

Winter opening times can differ from summer ones, and some of the smaller museums are open only in the summer half-year. Churches are sometimes closed over the lunch break. Since the shops are not subject to laws regarding business hours they have differing closing times in the evenings, but most shut on Monday mornings. And there is always fresh bread available on Sundays!

Entrance fees, even for the simplest attractions, are almost always high. You will need to set aside a generous amount for this purpose when calculating how much a visit to Normandy will cost.

Parking in towns

Since many places, even the smaller ones, have made pedestrian precincts of their Old Towns or town centres, it is not always easy to make your way around them by car or to be confident of finding an authorised parking place on the outskirts. If you have not parked correctly you will soon come to the notice of the French police and there will be a ticket on your windscreen and a fine to pay of 50, 100 or even 200 F.

Post and telephone

Post offices (*PTT*) are open from Mon. to Fri., 8 am–12 noon and 2–6 pm, Sat. from 8 am–12 noon. Stamps *(timbres)* are also available from tobacconists' shops. Remember when posting letters that one box is for the *département* you are in while the other, marked 'autres destinations', is for mail addressed abroad or to other parts of France.

Public telephones are identified by a black and yellow disc-shaped sign. Telephone cards, obtainable from post offices and *bars tabacs*, are widely used. Direct dialling abroad is possible from all telephone kiosks. When making a call abroad first dial the international service number (19) and wait for the tone before dialling the code (44 for the UK, 1 for the US and Canada; omit initial 0 from the area code). International calls are comparatively cheap, though hotels impose a surcharge of about 50%.

Public holidays

New Year: January 1st
Easter Monday
Labour Day: May 1st
Armistice Day (1945): May 8th
Ascension Day
Whit Monday
National holiday (Bastille Day):
   July 14th
Feast of the Assumption: August 15th
All Saints' Day: November 1st
Armistice Day (1918):
   November 11th
Christmas: December 25th

Restaurants

Since most restaurants are closed on one or two days a week and for at least one holiday a year this guide gives the telephone numbers of those mentioned. If you plan to take up our suggestions – they include only a tiny proportion of the establishments of every category which might be recommended – you should check with the restaurant beforehand even if you don't necessarily want to make a firm booking.

This sign indicates a recommended restaurant. Those listed tend to be the more expensive sort which will satisfy the more exacting type of customer. Some, however, are restaurants serving homely food at reasonable prices, and hotel restaurants of dependable quality are also included.

Station restaurants in France are not generally places to avoid; indeed they are usually very reliable and quite often occupy excellent premises. The ones listed satisfy both these criteria.

Tipping

A service charge (*service compris* or *s.c.*) is included by law in France in all hotels and restaurants. It is customary to round small amounts upwards but not to give an additional tip.

Touring by car

Vehicles travel on the right. Seat belts must be worn at all times. Motorists should carry the following: a nationality plate fixed to the back of the car; a warning triangle (unless car has hazard lights); spare sets of bulbs for all lights.

Priority: The old system, whereby traffic entering a road from the right had priority (*priorité à droite*), no longer applies, traffic on major roads now having priority (as does traffic already on roundabouts). However, signs will occasionally indicate exceptions (for example at some roundabouts) and drivers should familiarise themselves with these signs.

Speed limits: in built-up areas 50 kph (31 mph); outside built-up areas 90 kph (56 mph), but 80 kph (50 mph) in rain; on dual carriageways 110 kph (68 mph), but 100 kph (62 mph) in rain; on motorways 130 kph (81 mph), but 110 kph (68 mph) in rain. Drivers who have held a licence for less than one year: 90 kph maximum.

Documents: In addition to a valid driving licence and vehicle registration certificate it is advisable for motorists to obtain an international 'green card' insurance certificate.

Filling stations in country areas are often few and far between, or so modestly equipped that it is easy to miss them. Many close at lunch-time. Stations selling lead-free petrol (*essence sans plomb*) can be found in most towns and on motorways.

Important addresses
Diplomatic addresses

British Embassy
35 Rue du Faubourg St-Honoré
75008 Paris; tel. 1 42 66 91 42

US Embassy
2 Av Gabriel
75008 Paris; tel. 1 42 96 12 02

Canadian Embassy
35 Av Montaigne
75008 Paris; tel. 1 47 23 01 01

Australian Embassy
4 Rue Jean Rey
75724 Paris; tel. 1 45 75 62 00

New Zealand Embassy
7 ter Rue Léonard de Vinci
75116 Paris; tel. 1 45 00 24 11

Irish Embassy
4 Rue Rude
75116 Paris; tel. 1 45 00 20 87

Tourist information

In UK
French Government Tourist Office
178 Piccadilly
London WIV OAL; tel. 071 499 6911

French Railways
179 Piccadilly
London W1V OBA; tel. 071 493 4451

In USA
French Government Tourist Office
610 Fifth Avenue
New York NYC 10021

In France
Larger towns and smaller ones with tourist interest have a *Syndicat d'Initiative* (tourist office). Here you will find an abundance of brochures about anything and everything, from tourist routes to restaurants, hotels and festivals, regional museums and nature parks, the town itself, the surrounding area and the whole *département*. Many hotels also keep a supply of tourist information.

RAC
RAC Motoring Services Ltd
RAC House
PO Box 100
South Croydon CR2 6XW;
tel. 081 686 2525

French national motoring organisations
Automobile Club de France
6–8 Place de la Concorde
75008 Paris; tel. 1 42 65 34 70

Association Française des Automobilistes
9 Rue Anatole de la Forge
75017 Paris; tel. 1 42 27 82 00

Useful words and phrases

Although English is fairly widely understood in established tourist areas, the visitor will undoubtedly find a few words and phrases of French very useful.

please	s'il vous plaît
thank you (very much)	merci (bien)
yes/no	oui/non
excuse me	pardon
do you speak English?	parlez-vous anglais?
I do not understand	je ne comprends pas
good morning	bonjour
good evening	bonsoir
good night	bonne nuit
goodbye	au revoir
how much?	combien?
I should like	je voudrais
a room with private bath	une chambre avec bain
the bill, please! (in hotel)	la note, s'il vous plaît
(in restaurant)	l'addition
everything included	tout compris
when?	à quelle heure?
open	ouvert
shut	fermé
where is . . . street?	où se trouve la rue . . . ?
the road to . . . ?	la route de . . . ?
how far is it to . . . ?	quelle est la distance à . . . ?
to the left/right	à gauche/à droite
straight on	tout droit
post office	le bureau de poste
railway station	la gare
town hall	l'hôtel de ville/la mairie
exchange office	le bureau de change
police station	le commissariat/la poste de police
public telephone	la cabine téléphonique
tourist information office	l'office de tourisme/
	le syndicat d'initiative

doctor	le médecin	0 zéro
chemist	le pharmacien	1 un/une
toilet	la toilette	2 deux
ladies	dames	3 trois
gentlemen	messieurs	4 quatre
engaged	occupé	5 cinq
free	libre	6 six
entrance	l'entrée	7 sept
exit	la sortie	8 huit
today/tomorrow	aujourd'hui/demain	9 neuf
Sunday/Monday	dimanche/lundi	10 dix
Tuesday/Wednesday	mardi/mercredi	11 onze
Thursday/Friday	jeudi/vendredi	12 douze
Saturday/holiday	samedi/jeu de congé	20 vingt
		50 cinquante
		100 cent

Original German text: Wolfgang and Franziska Müller-Härlin. Translation: Wendy Bell
Series editor, English edition: Jane Rolph

© Verlag Robert Pfützner GmbH, München. Original German edition

© Jarrold Publishing, Norwich, Great Britain 1/91. English language edition worldwide

Published in the US and Canada by Hunter Publishing, Inc.,
300 Raritan Center Parkway, Edison NJ 08818

Illustrations: B. Bloomfield pages 1, 4, 47 both; J. Allan Cash Ltd pages 41, 42; Douglas Dickins
pages 7, 60, 88; Dennis Hughes-Gilbey pages 57, 74, 76; French Government Tourist Office
pages 15, 22, 34, 37, 38; R. Moss pages 25, 26, 27, 28, 29, 30, 32; C. Oldridge pages 3, 52 top,
53, 54, 63, 81; World Pictures pages 5, 44, 45, 69.

The publishers have made every endeavour to ensure the accuracy of this publication but can
accept no responsibility for any errors or omissions. They would, however, appreciate notification
of any inaccuracies to correct future editions.

Printed in Italy

ISBN 0–7117–0477–5